THE POETIC WORLD

IN A DREAM WORLD YOU GET HURLED
 WHEN YOU ENTER THE POETIC MIND
  A DELIGHT OF DREAM AND WISDOM WORLD,
   A FLOW OF EXCITING WORDS
    THE BEGINING TO ELEVATE YOUR SOUL
     THE BEAUTY WITHIN THE BEAUTY
      THEY ARE RHYTHMATIC NOT A DROLL,

by frauke danker

SHARE THE DELIGHT WITH THE PEOPLE
 LET THEM FEEL THE HEALING POWER OF EACH WORD
  THE OVERFLOW OF EMOTIONS INSIDE YOU
   TO EMBARK ON THE JOURNEY THAT HAS BEEN STIRRED,
    STIMULATING YOUR INTEREST AND ENJOYMENT
     AT PEACE MAYBE IN A CORNER OF YOUR HEART
      THE ENJOYMENT OF THE IMAGINARY
       YOUR HAPPY TO READ POEMS YOU DID START

BY CATHIE MARTIN

DARK ANGELS PRODUCTIONS

HI, IF YOU WANT TO PURCHASE ANY OF THE POETIC BOOKS FEATURED ON THE BACK OF THIS BOOK PLEASE FEEL FREE TO GO TO

www.waterstones.co.uk
http://darkangelsandprattcomics.wordpress.com
https://taxtor41.wixsite.com/darkangels

cathie martin on facebook
or email me..taxtor41@uwclub.net

Copyright (c) by Cathie and Chow Martin September 2021 All rights reserved printed by www.clocbookprint.co.uk

INTRODUCTION:

CATHIE A MULTIPLE SCLEROSIS SUFFERER HAS PUT TOGETHER THIS 148 PAGE BOOK OF A LOVELY COMPILATION OF WORDS AND PICTURES THAT WERE PICKED BY THE READERS ALSO SOME NEW POEMS THAT ARE EMOTIVE AND WILL EITHER MAKE YOU SMILE, SIGH, SHED A TEAR OR JUST GO AWE... THE WORK IS COMPLETELY UNIVERSAL SUITABLE FOR ANY AGE, LOTS OF COLOURS AND PICTURES FOR CHILDREN AND THE ADULTS WILL SEE A DEEPER SIDE.

I MUST GIVE GREAT THANKS TO MY HUSBAND CHOW MARTIN FOR DOING ALL THE LOVELY COVERS FOR ALL MY BOOKS AND ALSO SOME ADDITIONAL WORK, IF IT WERE NOT FOR CHOW PUSHING ME ONWARDS TO GET MY POETRY BOOKS PRINTED THERE WOULD NOT BE ANY TO SHARE WITH YOU THE READER. THANX DARLING CHOW XX

SO MY FRIENDS GET YOURSELF COMFY AND DELVE INTO THE INSPIRING WORDS AND PICTURES BY CATHIE MARTIN AND GUESTS.

Copyright (c) BY CATHIE AND CHOW MARTIN SEPTEMBER 2021 ALL RIGHTS RESERVED PRINTED BY www.clocbookprint.co.uk

CONTENTS: FROM BOOK AND ISBN NUMBER

#	Title	Author	Book	ISBN
1	LONG WINDING ROAD	BY CATHIE MARTIN	THE ROSE THAT CRIED	9781782806516
2	STOOD STANDING THERE	BY CATHIE MARTIN	WORDS	9781838537265
3	IN THE GARDEN	BY CHOW MARTIN	THE ROSE THAT CRIED	9781782805516
4	ANGEL OF STONE	BY CHOW MARTIN	THE ROSE THAT CRIED	9781782806516
5	A SHAM OF A LIFE, A GHOST OF THINGS THAT USED TO BE	BY CHOW MARTIN	WHAT THE BEES SAID TO ME	9781789729221
6	FRANKIE PICTURE	BY CHOW MARTIN.		
7	ADOPTED MUM	BY CATHIE MARTIN		
8	HAPPINESS	BY CATHIE MARTIN		
9	I WALK ALONE	BY CHOWE MARTIN	FLYING ON BROKEN WINGS	9781789260212
10	PUMPKIN HEAD	BY CATHIE MARTIN		
11	ODE TO CHIP	BY PAUL ELDRIDGE	WHAT THE BEES SAID TO ME	9781789729221
12	THANKS PAUL	BY CATHIE MARTIN ON BEHALF OF BASI		
13	WHEEL	BY CATHIE MARTIN	THE ROSE THAT CRIED	9781782806516
14	HAPPY VALENTINES DAY	BY ROMEO TANGHAL Sr	THE GENTLE ART OF POETR	9781800495436
15	MAMA	BY REBECCA EDBERG	THE GENTLE ART OF POETRY	9781800495436
16	OUR GLADYS	B Y CATHIE MARTIN		
17	THERE WERE THESE THREE BEARS	BY CATHIE AND CHOW MARTIN	FLYING ON BROKEN WINGS	9781789260212
18	LIGHTNING	BY CHOW MARTIN	FLYING ON BROKEN WINGS	9781789260212
19	IN YOUR HANDS I LEAVE MY HEART	BY JOHN O'DAY	FLYING ON BROKEN WINGS	9781789260212
20	INFECTIOUS	(c) BY ROMEO TANGHAL Sr		
21	WHERE WEEPING ROSES GO TO DIE	BY CHOW MARTIN	WHERE WEEPING ROSES GO TO DIE	9781782806523
22	WITNESS THE DEAD	BY CHOW MARTIN		
23	JOE AND HILARIE STATON	BY CATHIE MARTIN	WHAT THE BEES SAID TO ME	9781789729221
24	MY DOG IS A DOLPHIN	BY CHOW MARTIN		
25	BEAM ME UP	BY CATHIE MARTIN		
26	LOST	BY CHOW MARTIN	FLYING ON BROKEN WINGS	9781789260212
27	SAD EYES	BY CATHIE MARTIN		
28	GINGE	(C) BY AVRIL GRAY		
29	TEARFUL EYES	(C) BY SARA THOMSON	YESTERDAY I TAUGHT THE BIRDS TO SING	781782806530
30	TRUE LOVE	BY SUE BRYANT SHARPLES		
31	AND THE PUPPETS SHALL INHERIT THE EARTH	BY CHOW MARTIN	WORDS	9781838537265
32	SCARECROW	BY CATHIE MARTIN	THE GENTLE ART OF P OETRY	9781800495456
33	STICK	BY CHOW MARTIN	YESTERDAY I TAUGHT THE BIRDS TO SIN G	9781782806530
34	AT THE STROKE OF MIDNIGHT	BY CHOW MARTIN		
35	A SMALL DANCING LIGHT	BY CATHIE MARTIN	WORDS	9781838537265
36	ANGEL OF DEATH	BY CHOW MARTIN	AN ALIEN LIFE IN NORMAL TOWM	978178926482
37	OUR LIFE	BY AVRIL GRAY	THE GENTLE ART OF POETRY	9781800495456
38	WHAT THE BEES SAID TO ME	BY CHOW MARTIN	WHAT THE BEES SAID TO ME	9781789729221
39	LIFE AS A SOUND	BY CATHIE MARTIN	THE ROSE THAT CRIED	978178280651
40	THE MIRACULOUS STAIRCASE	BY CATHIE MARTIN	WORDS	9781838537265
41	OTTO	BY OTTO UND FRAUKE DANKER		
42	OTTO cntd....	BY OTTO UND FRAKE DANKRE		
43	ELVIS PIC	BY CHOW MARTIN	THE GENTLE ART OF POETRY	9781800495456
44	A TRIBUTE TO ELVIS PRESLEY	BY CATHIE MARTIN	THE GENTLE ART OF POETRTY	9781800495456
45	SOLDIER BOY	BY CATHIE MARTIN		
46	THE DREAM WEAVER	ART BY ROMEO TANGHAL Sr POEM BY CATHIE MARTIN		
47	DISABILITY	BY CATHIE AND CHOW MARTIN		
48	WORDS	BY CHOW MARTIN	WORDS	9781838537265
49	THE SILENT WAR (CORONAVIRUS)	BY CATHIE MARTIN	WORDS	9781838537265
50	VICTIM	BY CHOW MARTIN	REFLECTIONS IN A MURKY POOL	9781782806615
51	ALIENS	BY CHOW MARTIN	THE ROSE THAT CRIED	9781782806516
52	QUEEN OF FANTASY	ART BY ROMEO TANGHAL Sr POEM BY CATHIE MARTIN		
53	WALKING TOGETHER	BY CATHIE MARTIN	WHAT THE BEES SAID TO ME	9781789729221
54	PIC OF ELLENS GLEN EDINBURGH			
55	IN THE PAPERS	BY OTTO DANKER AND CATHIE MARTIN		
56	IN THE PAPERS cntd	BY OTTO DANERK AND CATHIE MARTIN		
57	WHO REMBERS WHEN......	INSPIRED BY CHOW MARTIN		
58	CONAN	INSPIRED BY CHOW MARTIN AND ROBERT E HOWARD	N AN ALIEN LIFE IN NORMAL TOWN	9781789269482
59	REMNANYS	BY ROSEMARIE ASHTON		
60	THE MEANING OF LIFE	BY CATHIE AND CHOW MARTIN	AN ALIEN LIFE IN NORMAL TOWN	9781789269482
61	LIFES QUESTION...	BY ROSEMARIE ASHTON	WHAT THE BEES SAID TO ME	9781789729221
62	THE BEAUTY OF LOVE	ART BY ROMEO TANGHAL Sr POEM BY CATHIE MARTIN		
63	WARM LOVE	BY CATHIE MARTIN		
64	I LAUGHED AND I LAUGHED	BY CATHIE MARTIN		
65	BULLY	BY TONI BEEDLE		
66	STUPIDITY	BY CATHIE MARTIN		
67	LIGHTHOUSE	BY CATHIE MARTIN	WHAT THE BEES SAID TO ME	9781789729221
68	SO POWERFUL	BY CHOW MARTIN	FYING ON BROKEN WINGS	9781789260212

#	Title	Author	Collection	ISBN
69	DON'T CRY FOR ME	BY CATHIE MARTIN	WHAT THE BEES SAID TO ME	9781789729221
70	AGED AND IN LOVE	BY CATHIE MARTIN		
71	I WANNA BE	BY CATHIE MARTIN	FLYING ON BROKEN WINGS	9781789260212
72	POEMS FOR THE PEOPLE	BY CATHIE MARTIN		
73	ONE	BY REBECCA HEDBERG		
74	DA DE DA DEE DA	BY BRIAN SMITH		
75	DIFFERENCES	BY CATHIE MARTIN		
76	TOILET ROLL	BY CATHIE MARTIN	THE GENTLE ART OF POETR	Y9781800495345
77	A LOADED DICE	BY MICHAEL NETZER	AN ALIEN LIFE IN NORMAL TOWN	9781789269489
78	HELL	BY CHOW MARTIN		
79	GLOBAL	BY CHOW MARTIN	WHAT THE BEES SAID TO ME	9781789729221
80	A GOOD MAN IS HARD TO FIND	BY CHOW AND CATHIE MARTIN		
81	ANIMAL FONDNESS	BY CATHIE MARTIN AND CHOW MARTIN		
82	THE HORROR	BY CATHIE MARTIN		
83	A TIGER, A TIGER	(C) SARA THOMSON 1999	YESTERDAY I TAUGHT THE BIRDS TO SING	9781782806530
84	COMIC BOOK LIFE	BY CATHIE MARTIN	WHAT THE BEES SAID TO ME	9781789729221
85	SADNESS	BY CATHIE MARTIN	THE ROSE THAT CRIED	9781782806516
86	ALONE IN THE PARK	BY CATHIE MARTIN	THE ROSE THAT CRIIED	9781782806516
87	WAITING	BY CHOW MARTIN	YESTERDAY I TAUGHT THE BIRDS TO SING	9781782806530
88	THE HAND (tribute to Jack 'King' Kirby	BY CATHIE MARTIN	WORDS	9781838537265
89	I'M GOING TO DIE I'M AFRAID OF THE DARK	BY CATHIE MARTIN		
90	I LIVED, I LIVED	BY CHOW MARTIN	WHAT THE BEES SAID TO ME	9781789729221
91	MARY KINGS' CLOSE	BY CATHIE MARTIN	WORDS	9781838537265
92	OOZUM IS SAYING BYE BYE	BY CATHIE MARTIN		
93	TRIBBLES TRIBUTE	BY CATHIE MARTIN	WORDS	9781838537265
94	DEATH ROW JETHRO	BY CATHIE MARTIN	THE ROSE THAT CRIED	9781782806516
95	BABY WENT ROCK-A-BYE	BY CATHIE MARTIN		
96	HERO	BY CATHIE MARTIN		
97	EDINBURGH DUNGEON	BY CATHIE MARTIN	WHAT THE BEES SAID TO ME	.9781789729221
98	PUSSYCAT	BY CATHIE MARTIN	WHAT THE BEES SAID TO ME	9781789729221
99	VISITOR	BY CATHIE MARTIN	FLYING ON BROKEN WING	9781789260212
100	THE SCARE WITHIN	BY CATHIE MARTIN.		
101	SANTA	BY CHOW MARTIN	AN LIEN LIFE IN NORMAL TOWN	9781789269482
102	AS THE FLOODING HELL CAME	(C) BY FRAUKE DANKER		
103	BABY BABY BUT WHAT'S INSIDE	BY CHOW MARTIN	AN ALIEN LIFE IN NORMAL TOWN	9781789269482
104	WHO ARE YOU?	BY colin hopkins .	YESTERDAY I TAUGHT THE BIRDS TO SING	9781782806530
105	THE ACRASIAL SPIRIT	BY CATHIE MARTIN		
106	EXPLOSIVE EXPRESSION OF LOVE	ART BY ROMEO TANGHAL Sr POEM BY CATHIE MARTIN		
107	YESTERDAY I TAUGHT THE BIRDS TO SING	BY CHOW MARTIN	YESTERDAY I TAUGHT THE BIRDS TO SING	9781782806530
108	LOVE YOUR FEATHERED FRIENDS	BY CATHIE MARTIN		
109	AT LAST	BY UNKNOWN		
110	A FORTUNE OF GOLD	BY CATHIE MARTIN		
111	THE BEES IN THE KNOW	BY CATHIE MARTIN	WHAT THE BEES SAID TO ME	9781789729221
112	FROZEN TEARS	BY CATHIE MARTIN		
113	POOCH	ART BY PAUL ELDTIDGE POEM BY CATHIE MARTIN		
114	HAPPY MERRY TIME	BY AVRIL GRAY		
115	INSIDE MY HEAD	POEM BY CATHIE MARTIN ART BY CHOW MARTIN		
116	TALK TO ME DAWGGIE	BY CATHIE MARTIN INSPIRED BY CHOW MARTIN		
117	GO TELL YOUR MOTHER ALL ABOUT IT	BY CATHIE MARTIN INSPIRED BY CHOW MARTIN		
118	GREYFRIARS BOBBY	BY CATHIE MARTIN	AN ALIEN LIFE IN NORMAL TOWN	9781789269482
119	GREY FRIARS BOBBY PICTURE			
120	WAITING FOR THE END	BY CATHIE AND CHOW MARTIN		
121	MY TIGER LOVE	BY CATHIE MARTIN		
122	OUR TIME TOGETHER	BY CATHIE MARTIN		
123	EVERYTHING MUST END	BY CATHIE MARTIN		
124	HOKAY BOYS!!	BY CATHIE MARTIN		

(C) COPYRIGHT BY CATHIE MARTIN AND CHOW MARTIN SEPTEMBER 2021 ALL RIGHTS RESERVED
PRINTED BY WWW.CLOCKBOOKPRINT.CO.UK

LONG WINDING ROAD

I FOLLOW THE ROAD
WHEREVER IT MAY GO
WHERE WILL I END UP
I DON'T KNOW,
A WIDE OPEN SPACE
WITH LOTS TO SEE
A LOVELY BLUE SKY
I FEEL FREE,
THE WIND IN MY FACE
BLOWING THROUGH MY HAIR
I'M ALONE IN THE WORLD
WITH NO-ONE TO CARE,
ANIMALS, FLOWERS
A LOVELY SWEET SMELL
FOLIAGE AND GRASS
LOTS OF COLOURS AS WELL,
IT ALL MAKES UP
A BEAUTIFUL LAND
I THINK OF PEOPLE
WALKING HAND IN HAND,
SHARING AND CARING
SPREADING LOVE HERE AND THERE
BUT I'M ALONE IN THE WORLD
WITH NO-ONE TO CARE.

BY CATHIE MARTIN

STOOD STANDING THERE

"GOOD MORNING TEACHER
I'M WILLING TO LEARN
ASK ME ANY QUESTION
I KNOW I'M JUST A BAIRN,
IF I ANSWER CORRECTLY
CLEVER I WILL BE
YOU CAN PRAISE ME UP
TO MY PARENTS ABOUT ME,"
"OKAY MASTER CHOW
TO GIVE ANSWER TO WHAT I ASK
COME UP HERE BESIDE ME
STAND IN FRONT OF THE CLASS,
OKAY ANSWER ME THIS THEN
DOES A SPIRAL GO ON FOREVER
I'M SURE YOU KNOW THE ANSWER
BECAUSE YOU ARE SO CLEVER,"
"A SPIRAL OR LATERALUS
MY ANSWER WILL BE TERSE
IT IS INFINATE
IT REFERS TO THE UNIVERSE,
A SYMBOL OF GROWTH
WELL THAT IS MY NOTION
IT WILL NEVER END
IT IS DEVELOPMENT AND EVOLUTION,"
"IF YOU TRAVEL FROM A TO B
ALWAYS STOPPING HALF WAY
WILL YOU GET WHERE YOU WANT
OR WILL YOU BE THERE ALL DAY,"
"ALWAYS STOPPING HALF WAY
YOUR JOURNEY WILL GO ON AND ON
YOU'LL NEVER REACH YOUR DESTINATION
YOU NEVER WILL BE DONE,"
"THAT WAS VERY GOOD CHOW
YOU ANSWERED THAT WITH EASE
THE BELL WILL BE RINGING SOON
NOW TAKE YOUR SEAT PLEASE"

BY CATHIE MARTIN

IN THE GARDEN

I DWELL IN THE GARDEN HOLDING ON TO MY ROD
I SEE WONDERFUL LIFE ALL AROUND ME, MAKES ME FEEL SO CLOSE TO GOD

SO QUICKLY THE GRASS GROWS SO IT APPEARS TO ME
GREEN ALL AROUND ME AS FAR AS I CAN SEE

I'M HAPPY IN MY PLACE SO HAPPY AS CAN BE
SO CONTENT AND SERENE THERE CAN BE NO ONE AS TRANQUIL AS ME

BEING PART OF THE GARDEN FILLS MY WHOLE HEART WITH GLEE
I'M A GNOME, I'M FISHING FOR ALL THE WORLD TO SEE

BY CHOW MARTIN

ANGEL OF STONE

YOU PUT ME HERE
 YOU LAID ME IN PLACE
  I KNOW WHO YOU ARE
   I KNOW YOUR FACE

I CAN'T SPEAK
 I'M MADE OF STONE
  I'M PUT OUT HERE
   ALL ON MY OWN

IN THE DARK OF THE NIGHT
 OR IN THE LIGHT OF DAY
  I'VE GOT LOTS OF THINGS
   THAT I NEED TO SAY

BUT THE DIALOUGE WON'T COME
 MY LIPS ARE MUTE
  NO WORDS MAY I UTTER
   NO TONGUE TO DISPUTE

BY CHOW MARTIN

A SHAM OF LIFE, A GHOST OF THINGS THAT USED TO BE

MORE THAN A MONSTER
LESS THAN A MAN
TO SEE ME IS TO FEAR ME
SINCE IT ALL BEGAN,
A WELL MEANING DOCTOR
BODY PARTS HE DID USE
HE'D ALSO VISIT ABATTOIRS
TENDONS OF ANIMALS HE DID CHOOSE,
PUT ME TOGETHER
IN A JIGSAW PUZZLE FOR REAL
ONCE HE PULLED THE LEVER
THE CONSEQUENCES HE MUST DEAL,
ELECTRICITY DID FLOW THROUGH ME
THE GIVER OF LIFE IT BE
IF FRANKENSTEIN BE MY FATHER
MY MOTHER IS LIGHTNING YOU SEE,
A PIECEMEAL MADE OF BODY PARTS
NO GOOD CAN COME TO ME
A MISHAPPEN CREATURE
A MOCKERY OF MAN I BE,
I ONLY WANT TO BE ACCEPTED
IT MUST BE PLAIN TO SEE
ALONE, I FEEL DESPERATE
HUMANITY WILL NOT ACCEPT ME,
MY BONES THEY REEK OF HISTORY
THAT IS NOT ME
THE GRAVE I SEEK, THE GRAVE I CRAVE
I WANT TO BE UNBORN,
WHEN I SHUFFLE OF MY JIGSAW SPIRIT
NO ONE LIVING SHALL MOURN
THE FROZEN NORTH MY HOME NOW
AIMLESSLY I WONDER NOW,
THE COLD I KNOW WILL CLAIM ME
PEACE WILL OVER COME AND HOW.

(by mr chow martin)

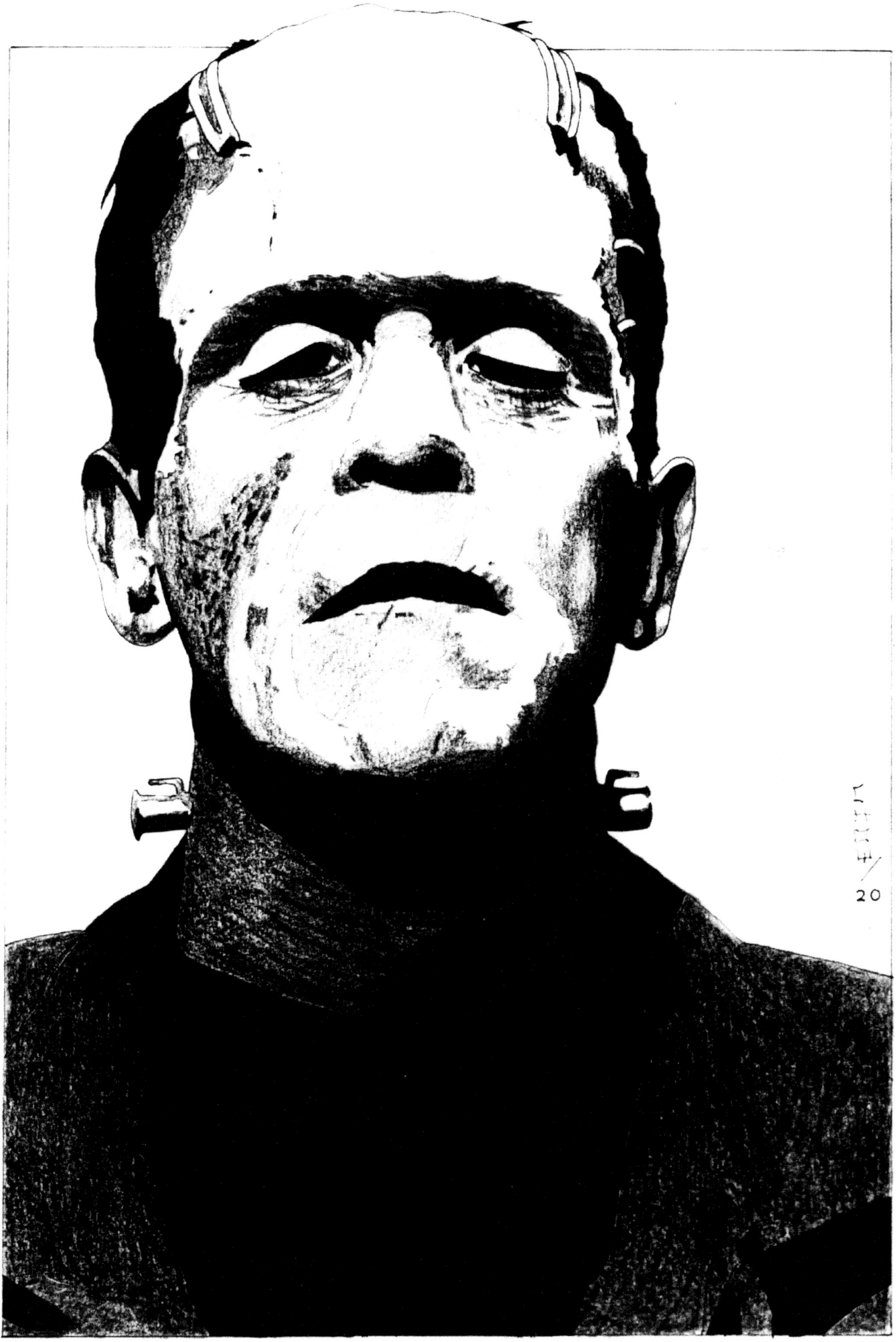

ADOPTED MUM

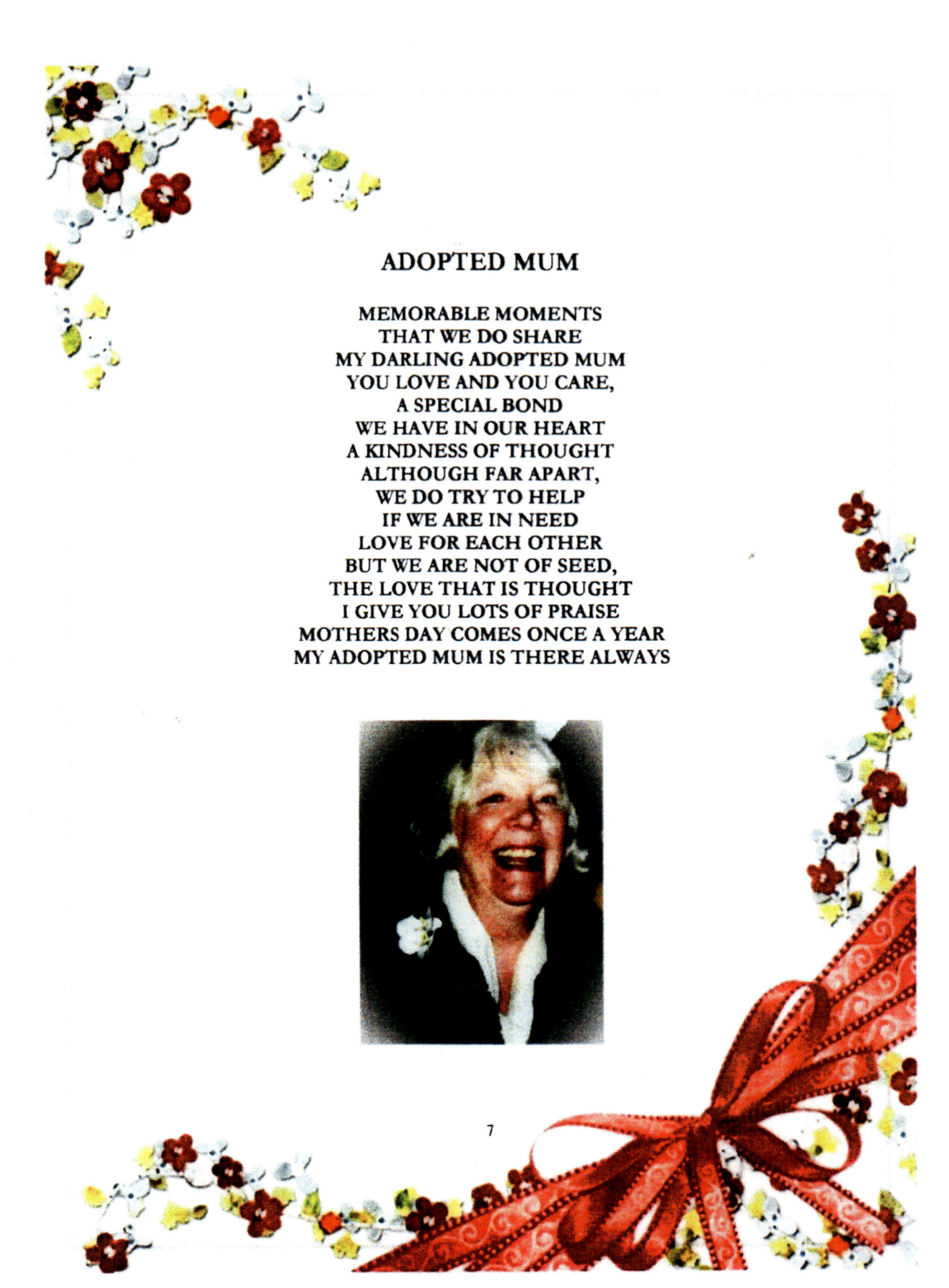

MEMORABLE MOMENTS
THAT WE DO SHARE
MY DARLING ADOPTED MUM
YOU LOVE AND YOU CARE,
A SPECIAL BOND
WE HAVE IN OUR HEART
A KINDNESS OF THOUGHT
ALTHOUGH FAR APART,
WE DO TRY TO HELP
IF WE ARE IN NEED
LOVE FOR EACH OTHER
BUT WE ARE NOT OF SEED,
THE LOVE THAT IS THOUGHT
I GIVE YOU LOTS OF PRAISE
MOTHERS DAY COMES ONCE A YEAR
MY ADOPTED MUM IS THERE ALWAYS

BY CATHIE MARTIN

HAPPINESS

THE FUN OF LAUGHTER
YOU MAY SHED A TEAR
THE GIGGLES ARE CATCHY
TO ALL THOSE WHO ARE NEAR,
IT BRIGHTENS THE DAY
INFECTIOUS AS THEY ARE
YOUR CHUCKLE MUSCLES ARE WORKING
IT MAY SEEM BIZARRE,

WHAT IS THE REASON
NO JOKE WAS TOLD
THE ENJOYMENT OF LIFE
FOR THE WORLD TO HOLD,
A SIMPLE LITTLE GESTURE
MEANS A LOT TO SOME
A MEDICINE TO SHARE
INFECTED' THE WORLD WILL BECOME

BY CATHIE MARTIN

I WALK ALONE

I HAVE NO FUTURE
 ALL THAT IS PAST
  MY LIFE IS EMPTY
   I WALK ALONE

IN THIS WORLD
 WHAT IS LIFE
  NO-ONE TO LOVE
   I WALK ALONE

I THINK OF TOMORROW
 WHAT DOES IT HOLD
  NOTHING FOR ME
   I WALK ALONE

I PRAY TO THE LORD
 TO SHOW ME THE WAY
  I AM SO LOST
   I WALK ALONE

BY CHOW MARTIN

PUMPKIN HEAD

HAPPY IN THE GARDEN
GROWING IN THE WARM WEATHER
BUT IN THE COLD MONTHS
WE'RE ALL GATHERED UP TOGETHER,
WE ARE TAKEN AWAY
TO GET OUR FACES FIXED
SO YOU'LL TAKE US OUT
FOR THE HALLOWEEN TRICKS,
SO SHAPE ALL OUR FACES
SPOON OUT OUR MOUTH, NOSE AND EYES
WE'LL TRY SCARE THE PEOPLE
THEY'LL GET LAUGHS, SCREAMS AND CRIES,
ALL NIGHT LONG
OUR FACES WILL SHINE
ALL TO HAVE FUN
AT THIS *SCARY* TIME

BWAAHAHAHA

BY CATHIE MARTIN

Ode to Chip

I'll never forget our walks,
and our late night strolls with Bold.
I'll never forget your smile,
and the happiness that could travel a mile.
I'll never forget the huffs and gruffs of joy,
as I wrestle with the big brown boy,
I'll never forget the tugs of war,
hog the biggest bed that you can, Chippers...
Let nobody forget your big brown bear roar.

BY MR PAUL ELDRIDGE

THANKS PAUL

THANK YOU FOR THE CARING
ALL THE LOVE YOU GIVE TO ME
YOUR A TERRIFIC PERSON PAUL
I'M GLAD I BELONG TO THEE,
I LIKE MY FREEDOM
I ENJOY MY COMFORT TOO
I LIKE CURLING UP AT NIGHT
KNOWING I'M NOT FAR FROM YOU

BY BASIL

WHEEL

THE WHEEL OF FUN
YOU HAVE IN YOUR DREAMS
WHAT IS THE REASON
WHAT DOES IT MEAN

        WITH AN ANGRY SKY
        AND A DRY LAND
        NO LEAVES ON THE TREES
        TO TOUCH WITH YOUR HAND

A STRANGE FEELING IN YOUR HEAD
YOU DON'T KNOW WHERE YOU ARE
YOU CAN SEE OPEN WATER
YOU SEE A BRIGHT STAR

        YOUR IN A TURMOIL
        DIZZY WITH THOUGHT
        LOSING YOUR BEARINGS
        YOUR LOSING THE PLOT

PANIC AND STRUGGLE
YOU THINK YOU WILL FALL
WANTING SAFE GROUND
YOU GIVE A LOUD CALL

        YOUR COMING BACK
        YOU KNOW WHERE YOU ARE
        BUT WHAT ARE YOU HOLDING
        YOUR CLUTCHING A STAR

BY CATHIE MARTIN

Happy Valentine's Day.

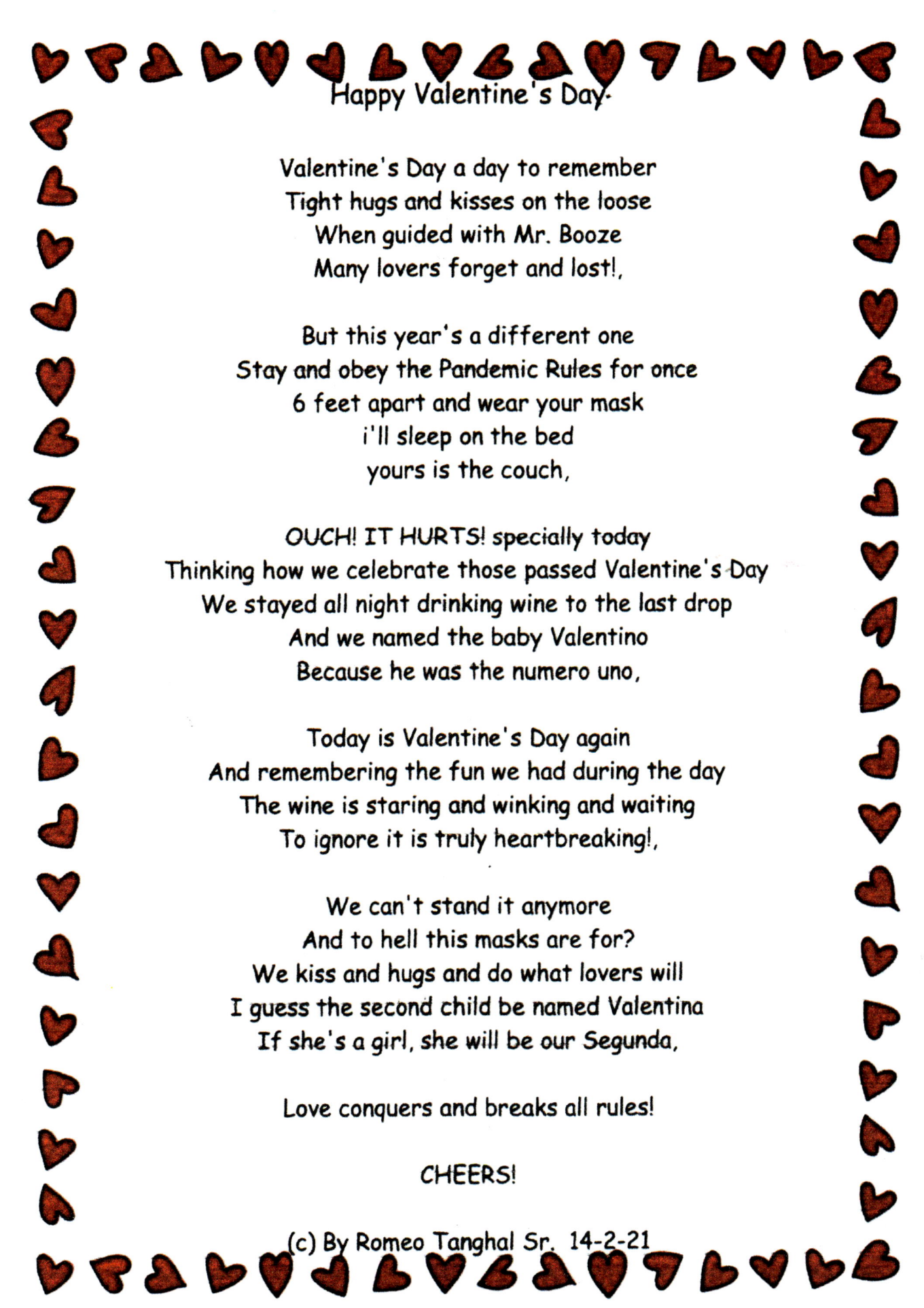

Valentine's Day a day to remember
Tight hugs and kisses on the loose
When guided with Mr. Booze
Many lovers forget and lost!,

But this year's a different one
Stay and obey the Pandemic Rules for once
6 feet apart and wear your mask
i'll sleep on the bed
yours is the couch,

OUCH! IT HURTS! specially today
Thinking how we celebrate those passed Valentine's Day
We stayed all night drinking wine to the last drop
And we named the baby Valentino
Because he was the numero uno,

Today is Valentine's Day again
And remembering the fun we had during the day
The wine is staring and winking and waiting
To ignore it is truly heartbreaking!,

We can't stand it anymore
And to hell this masks are for?
We kiss and hugs and do what lovers will
I guess the second child be named Valentina
If she's a girl, she will be our Segunda,

Love conquers and breaks all rules!

CHEERS!

(c) By Romeo Tanghal Sr. 14-2-21

Mama

I inhaled my first breath
and that's because of you

I saw my first tomorrow
and into the future we flew

My first steps and my first words
you saw and heard it all

I your arms I was lying safe
and you would never let me fall

I admire your strenght and courage
and you will never be far

Nothing can ever tear us apart
because you my life force are

You gave me everything I needed
I will forever greatful be

I can never repay you for the gift of life
or the gift of you and me

BY REBECCA HEDBERG

OUR GLADYS

FOR GLADYS DAVIS M.B.E

YOU'VE BEEN HERE ALL THE TIME
SUCH A DEAREST FRIEND OF OURS
YOUR NICE LIKE THE SWEET SMELLING
LOVELY ROSE FLOWERS,

WITH CONFIDENCE AND DEDICATION
YOUR HELP IS ALWAYS THERE
YOUR A LOVELY PERSON
PEOPLE WHO KNOW YOU CARE

BY CATHIE MARTIN

THERE WERE THESE THREE BEARS

YOU FEEL ALONE IN THE WORLD
WITH NOT A FRIEND
QUIET AND DISABLED
YOU MAY NEVER MEND

BUT YOU CAN DREAM
THAT LEAVES A TEAR
YOU DREAM OF ANIMALS
DANCING WITH A BEAR

THE BEAR KNOWS YOU ARE SAD
IT'S FUNNY BUT IT'S TRUE
HE APPROACHES YOU SOFTLY
AND BRINGS HIS BROTHERS TOO

THEY SURROUND YOU
WITH HAPPINESS AROUND
YOUR HAPPY AND LIVING
DANCING TO THEIR SOUND

GIVING YOU A SMILE
BUT YOU HAVE TO LEAVE
AWAKENING....WAS IT TRUE
IT'S WHAT YOU PERCEIVE

BY CATHIE AND CHOW MARTIN

In Your Hands I Leave My Heart

As I put pen to paper
my thoughts belong to you
I pray to the god each night
to help me see this through...
Someday I hope to be with you
never more to part
until then my darling children
in your hands I leave my heart...
Inside I feel so empty
because you're not within
my touch, but, believe me when I
tell you kids, I love you very much...
Help me through this nightmare lord
show me the way home,
point me in the right direction
don't let my childrren be alone...
I love them so very much
they mean the world to me,
after all, I am their mother
with them I only want to be...
I want to share their problems
be there when they shed a tear,
I want to share their happiness
and joy year after year...
So watch me when I'm falling lord
keep strong my aching heart,
keep that bond between us strong
despite the miles apart...

LIGHTNING

UP FROM THE GROUND
TOGETHER UNITE
WE SHALL BE AS ONE
LIGHTING THE SKY O' SO BRIGHT

FAST AS THE EYE CAN SEE
IN SECONDS BLISS
FOR YOU AND ME
BEWARE OF THE KISS

THE POWER WE HAVE
FOR ALL TO FEAR
WE DON'T LIVE LONG
BUT DON'T SHED A TEAR

ELECTRIAL FORCES
FROM ABOVE YOUR HEAD
IF ONE OF US STRIKES YOU
YOU WILL END UP DEAD

THE STORM IT RAGES
FOR ME NOT FOR YOU
THE SKY IS ANGRY
BUT WHAT CAN YOU DO

LIGHTNING WE ARE
THAT'S WHAT WE BE
WHEN THUNDERS AROUND
DON'T COME LOOKING FOR ME

BY CHOW MARTIN

INFECTIOUS

Smiling is infectious
You catch it like the flu

When someone smiled at me today
I started smiling too

I walked around the corner
And someone saw me grin

When he smiled I realised
I had passed it on to him

I thought about the smile
And then realised its worth

A single smile like mine
Could travel round the earth

So if you feel a smile begin
Don't leave it undetected

Start an epidemic
And get the world infected.

ROMEO TANGHAL Sr
(C) Romeo Tanghal Sr 7/3/21

WHERE WEEPING ROSES GO TO DIE...

I LIE HERE ALONE AS TIME PASSES BY
THE GRASS ABOVE ME REACHES FOR THE SKY
OH! WHY OH! WHY CANT I

I KNOW THE REASON IN TRUTH I DO...
I'M DEAD NOW DECAYING NOTHING I CAN DO

REGRETS COME TO ME...MY LIFE WAS A MESS
I LIVED A 'DEVIL MAY CARE' LIFE I COULDN'T CARE LESS

MY LIFE WAS GOOD MY LIFE WAS FAST
IT REALLY SEEMED LIKE IT WOULD ALWAYS LAST

MY COMPANIONS NOW ARE COLD AND DARK
I'M SO ALONE HERE IN THIS PARK

IF MY LIPS COULD TALK THAY'D SAY TO YOU
DONT BE A BAD PERSON, ALWAYS BE TRUE

BY MR CHOW MARTIN

WITNESS THE DEAD

WITNESS THE DEAD
    THE DEAD ARE NOT HERE
STORIES TO TELL
    THAT WE MUST HEAR,
THEIR LIVES MAYBE TRAGIC
    BUT WE HOLD THEM DEAR
THEY GAVE US SO MUCH
    THAT IS SO CLEAR,
WE MUST REMEMBER THE PAST
    FOR THE FUTURE IS SO UNCLEAR
WITNESS THE DEAD
    THEY ARE SO CLOSE, SO NEAR

BY CHOW MARTIN

JOE AND HILARIE STATON

JOE AND HILARIE STATON
HAVE BEEN TOGETHER FOR YEARS
THEY'VE NO DOUBT BEEN THROUGH
MANY SMILES AND MANY TEARS,

BEEN THROUGH THE GOOD
BEEN THROUGH THE BAD
HAVING THE HAPPY
AND SOMETIMES THE SAD,

SEEING THE DAYS THROUGH
WITH LOVING ESTEEM
LIVING A HAPPY LIFE
LIVING THEIR DREAM,

A LOVING COUPLE
WE ARE ALL HAPPY TO KNOW
WE LOOK IN WONDER AND ADMIRATION
HAPPINESS WE DO SHOW,

BY CATHIE MARTIN

MY DOG IS A DOLPHIN

MY DOG IS A DOLPHIN
HE LOVES TO COME AND PLAY
MY DOG IS A DOLPHIN
I'M WITH HIM ALL DAY,
HE'S ALWAYS PLEASED TO SEE ME
WE ALWAYS HAVE SUCH FUN
MY FRIEND THE DOLPHIN
WE ARE LIKE JUST ONE,
MY DOG IS A DOLPHIN
THERE'S NOT MANY KNOWN TO US ALL
MY FRIENDLY LITTLE PLAYMATE
COMES TO ME WHEN I CALL,
FETCHING TOYS THAT ARE THROWN FAR
WE SWIM AND JUMP ALL THE SAME
MY DOG IS A DOLPHIN
THAT'S WHAT I CALL HIM, THAT'S HIS NAME

BY CHOW MARTIN

BEAM ME UP

BEAM ME UP, TAKE ME AWAY
TO ANOTHER LAND
THE CULTURE, THE LIVES
I'LL START TO UNDERSTAND,
THE PROBLEMS THAT OCCUR
SHOW ME YOUR WAY
A FOREIGN BEING
I WILL WITH YOU STAY,
STRANGE FANTASTIC COLOURS
WONDEROUS LIVING
WE WILL COMBINE AS ONE
WE BELIEVE THIS IS HEAVEN,
THE FRIENDLINESS, THE SMILES
THE HELPFUL HAND
WE HOLD OUR HEAD UP
THE ALMIGHTY DO STAND,
NO-ONE IS DIFFERENT
WE ARE ALL AS ONE
BACK TO LIFES STAR
BACK.. WHERE IT BEGUN

BY CATHIE MARTIN

LOST

I AM SO LOST
  I DON'T KNOW WHO I AM
    I'VE LOST ALL KNOW HOW
      I AM GOING TO CRY

              WHAT TO DO
                OR WHERE TO GO
                  PLEASE HELP ME
                    COS' I DON'T KNOW

> WHO AM I?
> WHY DO I HURT SO?
> WHERE AM I?
> HOW DID I GET HERE?
> HOW DO I GET OUT OF HERE?

I WANT TO FIND MY WAY
  I WANT TO GO HOME
    BUT WHERE IS MY PLACE
      OR IS IT JUST SO

              MY FEELINGS ARE HURT
                I WON'T LET YOU SEE
                  I'VE LOST WHO I AM
                    I AM NO LONGER ME

BY CHOW MARTIN

SAD EYES

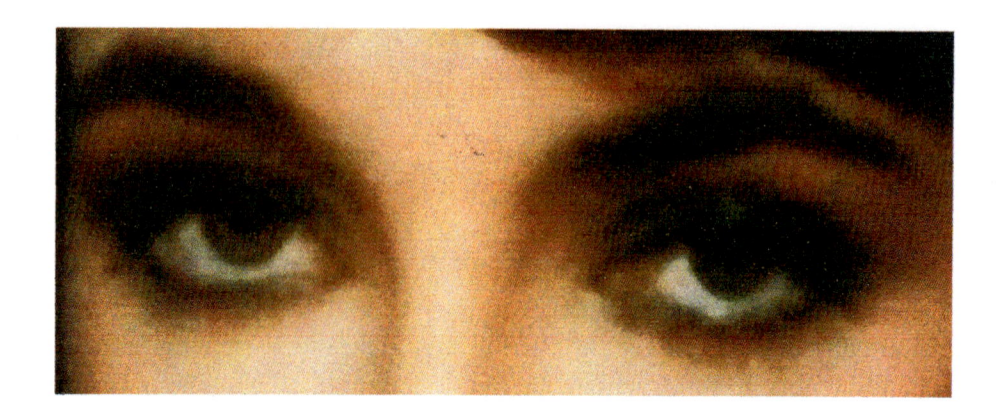

THE EYES ARE THE MIRROR TO YOUR SOUL
WHAT HIDES WITHIN YOU IS WOE
WHERE YOUR AT YOU DON'T KNOW
THE FEELINGS THAT HURT, THEY DO SO SHOW,
THE EYES TO ME DO SPEAK
INSIDE NO MORE STRONG, BUT SO WEAK
THE STRENGTH TO CARRY ON YOU SEEK
BUT THE OUTCOME IS DIRE, SO BLEAK,
THE BEAUTY OF LOVE IS AWAY
THE SKY NO LONGER BLUE TIS'ALL GREY
WHAT IS THERE FOR YOU TO DISPLAY
THE HURT, THE SORROW YOU DOWNPLAY,
YOU CAN'T TAKE IT ANYMORE, YOU GIVE IN
EARS OUT THERE TO ME PLEASE LISTEN
MY EYES CAN'T SMILE THEY CAN'T GRIN
MY STORY TO TELL I WILL BEGIN

BY CATHIE MARTIN

Ginge

Our beautiful adored ginger cat
For nineteen years you sat on the mat
You purred and played on many a day
And broke our hearts when you went away
The cat flap is still, the garden too
Oh Ginge wee darling, we so miss you

    (c) Avril Gray 2021

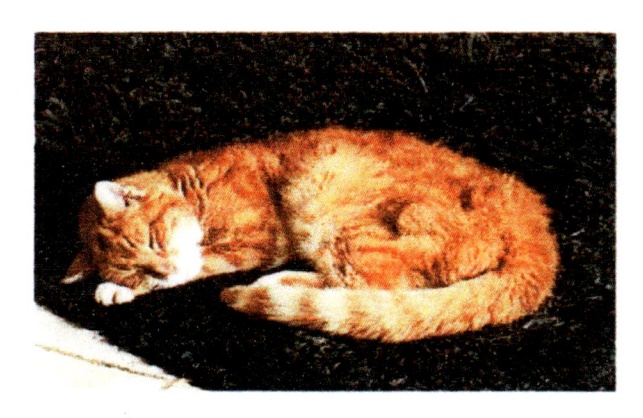

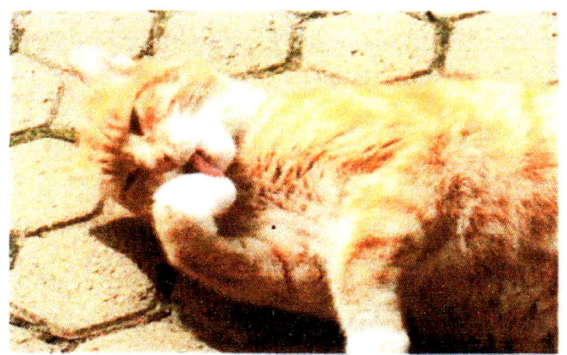

Tearful Eyes

Eyes of tears that can't flow.

But these tearful eyes will never show.

They will always hide like they're shy.

They make me wish I knew how to lie.

This mask of skin covers my face.

It makes me hide in that dark, empty place.

It hides my frown and creates a smile.

It makes these tearful eyes hide for a while.

There is a door in my mind I can't go through.

Where thoughts are stored that I can't get to.

The door is locked and I've lost the key.

I need these thoughts to set my tearful eyes free.

Feelings clogged deep in my heart.

These feelings slowly tearing my insides apart.

The secret behind them will always hide,

As long as these tearful eyes are deep inside.

Full eyes of tears

But just can't seem to flow.

Now these tearful eyes,

Will never ever show!!!!

©Sara Thomson 2005

TRUE LOVE

THE WEDDING OF TRUE LOVE FOREVER
THAT WILL LAST ALWAYS AND A DAY
NO END TO THE TRUENESS OF LOVING
THE HAPPY DAY THAT 'I LOVE YOU' WE SAY,
WE WILL TRAVEL TO THE END OF THE EARTH
WITH NEW BEGININGS TO BEGIN
TOM AND SUE WILL BE FOREVER
THEIR HEARTS LIKE THE BIRDS DO SING,
I HOLD DEEP YOUR LOVE MY DARLING
WITH YOU I SHALL ALWAYS BE
CHERISH IN THE TIME TOGETHER
I BELIEVE IN YOU, YOU BELIEVE IN ME,
I VOW TO BE YOUR PRINCESS DARLING
A PRINCE OF LOVE IN YOU I SEE
SPEND ALL THE SECONDS IN OUR LIFETIME
A HAPPY EVER AFTER IN TIME WE SHALL BE

BY SUE BRYANT-SHARPLES

AND THE PUPPETS SHALL INHERIT THE EARTH...

PEOPLE ARE THE PUPPETS OF THE POLITICIANS.

YOU DON'T BELIEVE EVERY WORD THEY SAY
BUT JUST ENOUGH TO VOTE THEM IN ANYWAY

THEY PULL THE STRINGS TO WIN YOUR VOTE
THE CHANCES OF VOTING WITH YOUR HEAD
IS ALL TOO REMOTE

YOU THINK YOU'VE WON WHEN YOU'VE
ALL BUT LOST
YOU CHEER YOU HOOT BUT O' THE COST

THE PIGS ARE IN THE PEN NOW, OH WHAT A
 MESS THEY'LL MAKE

YOU REALLY SHOULD KNOW BY THIS TIME THEY'RE
ALL JUST ON THE TAKE

YOU VOTED THEM IN, YOUR IN CHARGE YOU SAY
BUT THE EMPTY PROMISES HOW YOU WILL PAY

BEWARE THE ANIMAL FARM...

BY MR CHOW MARTIN

SCARECROW

STANDING IN THE FIELD
IS THE FUNNY SCARECROW
OUT THERE IN ALL WEATHERS
NO ONE KNOWS OF IT'S WOE,
IT'S WELL DRESSED UP
WITH A HAPPY LOOKING SMILE
WHAT DOES IT DO
COS' IT'S OUT THERE FOR A WHILE,
THE BIRDIES WILL GO AND VISIT
DO THEY TALK TO IT?? MAYBE
MIGHT SING IT A SONG
WE CAN'T HEAR WHAT THEY SAY,
OUT AT NIGHT IN THE COLD
AS THE MOON DOES SHINE
STILL LOOKS VERY DASHING
DRESSED UP LOOKING FINE,
IF I PLAY SOME MUSIC
WILL IT DANCE WITH ME
MAYBE IT IS HUNGRY
SHOULD I INVITE HIM IN FOR TEA,
TELL ME LITTLE SCARECROW
ARE YOU HAPPY TO BE
OUT IN THE FIELD
LOOKING AFTER IT FOR ME

BY CATHIE MARTIN

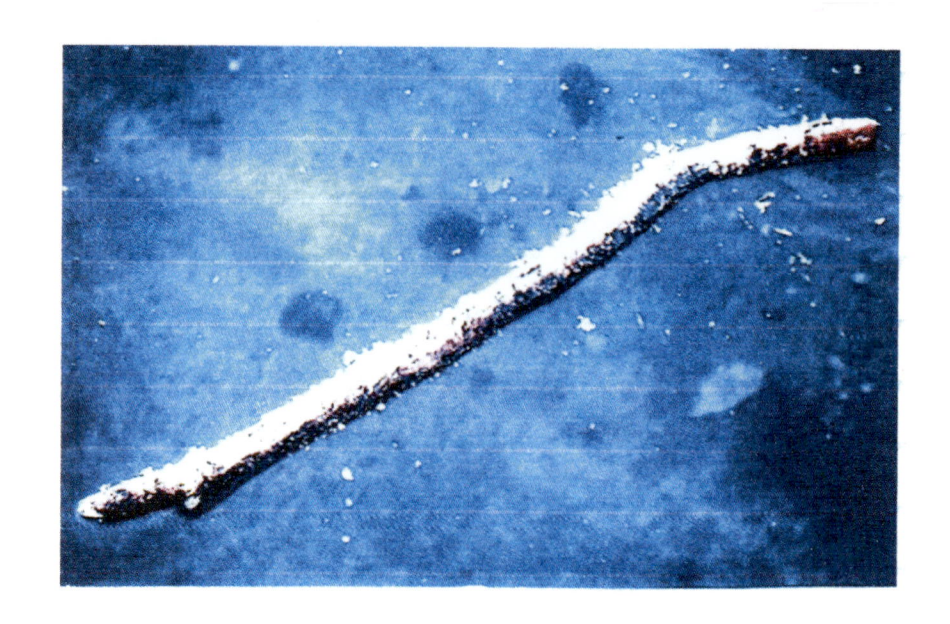

STICK

I'M IN A RACE
BUT I CARE NOT
WIN OR LOSE
I DON'T CARE TO CHOOSE

DOWN STREAM I GO
WET FROM HEAD TO TOE
MY DESTINY IS NOT MINE
NO, WILL I HAVE TO DECLINE?

TRAVEL I MUST
ON AN UNCERTAIN COURSE
THINGS THAT CAN HAPPEN
ONLY GET WORSE

UNDER THE BRIDGE
LIGHT SHOWING THROUGH
I'M A WINNER NOW
NO THANKS TO YOU

A STICK IN THE WATER
IS ALL I MAY BE
FREE FOREVER MORE
FROM THE LIKES OF THEE

PLACED HERE BY HUMANS
BUT WHAT CAN I DO
I'M A PAWN IN THIS GAME
THAT THE DO

BY MR CHOW MARTIN

AT THE STROKE OF MIDNIGHT

UP AT MIDNIGHT WITH PAINS IN THE HEAD
IN A FEW SHORT MOMENTS THIS MUM WOULD BE DEAD,

MY MOTHER FELT GIDDY, MY MOTHER FELT ILL
THE ROOM SWAM AROUND HER, SOON THERE
WOULD BE A KILL,

THE FLOOR RUSHED UP TO MEET HER AND
HER MOTHERLY THOUGHTS WERE NO MORE

THE KETTLE STARTED CRYING AS THE ELDERLY
WOMAN LAY THERE DIEING,

A STROKE OF BAD LUCK THE DOCTOR DID SAY
A JOKE OF BAD TASTE MUCH TO OUR DISMAY,

BURIED ON MONDAY, SAME DAY SHE WAS BORN
THEY CAME OUT IN FORCE, A GREAT WOMAN THEY DID MOURN,

SHE'LL BE MISSED BY MANY, BLESSED AS SHE WAS
THROUGH OUT HER LONG LIFE SHE DID RIGHT THE GOOD CAUSE

BY MR CHOW MARTIN

A
SMALL
DANCING
LIGHT
WITH
ME

THE LIGHT WITHIN
WILL BURN BRIGHT
THROUGH THE DAY
AND IN THE NIGHT,
AS LONG AS YOU LIVE
LIGHT SHALL BE THERE
BEING IN YOUR LIFE
GIVING YOU CARE,
THE LIGHT TAKES SHAPE
SHADOWS ALL AROUND
THE DANCING FIGURES
DON'T MAKE A SOUND,
THE SILENCE THE WARMTH
AS THE LIGHT DOES SWAY
THE HOPING, THE PRAYERS
AS IT FLICKERS AWAY,
BURNING SO QUIETLY
BURNING SO BRIGHT
THIS LITTLE FLICKER
THIS FLICKER OF LIGHT

BY CATHIE MARTIN

ANGEL OF DEATH

BIRD GOES TO CHURCH
TO REPENT HIS SINS
HE'S A BIRD OF PREY
THE CHURCH IS HIS SOLACE
REPENT I MUST
FOR KILLER I AM AND BE
I LIKE IT NOT WHAT I DO
MY SOUL I MUST SET FREE
I'M EVIL UNLIMIITED
BUT THAT'S NOT REALLY TRUE
THAT'S WHY I COME HERE LORD
TO PRAY UNTO YOU

IF LIVE I WILL
THEN DEATH MUST COME
I MUST REPENT
I AM NO SPECIAL ONE
I CLEATHE THROUGH THE AIR
THE FEATHERS DO FLY
KILL AS I MUST
I EVER DO SIGH
MY WINGS THEY BEAT
THE BEAT OF DEATH
I CAN HEAR A CALLING
DEATH DOES COMMETH
MY LIFE IS WHAT IT IS
THIS GIVES ME NO GLEE
I AM WHAT I AM
I'M A BIRD OF PRAY YOU SEE

BY CHOW MARTIN

OUR LIFE

At fourteen years old we had a vision
To own our own home was the big mission
Ten years later....what can I say
We bought a cracker in Dalgety Bay
We then had a bundle come home to our house
She wasn't very big but bigger than a mouse!
Best years of our lives were lived in the bay
Fond memories cherished along the way
The house and bundle were our pride and joy
Altho at times we couldn't afford a toy
Thatcher was in....we had to move
Back over to Nittin, didn't feel like a groove

Another precious bundle came into the fold
Before we knew it she was twenty years old

Our precious girls brought laughter and life
But one moved to London causing much strife
The bright lights of theatre she made in her life
Twenty years later she's become a wife

The other stayed home and thrived her way
Serving community, she's here to stay
home bird by admission loving her life
And now she has also become a wife

We made it, we built it, our forever home
Altho we love Nittin, we still like to Roam
Each day an adventure, a fabulous time
What more could we ask for in our prime

Fifty years later still joined at the hip
Let's pour a wee whiskey and have a wee sip

The future we know it yet to unfold
Grandchildren bring joy, or so we're told!
A fabulous life will be our acclaim
Forever fourteen without any shame

BY AVRIL GRAY

WHAT THE BEES SAID TO ME

IT'S TIME FOR HUMANITY
TO SET ITSELF FREE
IT'S TIME FOR US TO DO THINGS
THAT'S YOU AND ME,

THE EARTHS AT A TURNING POINT
THE TIME TO ACT IS NOW
AS YOU READ THIS POEM BOOK
IT'S TIME TO MAKE A VOW,

MOTHER EARTH HAS LOOKED AFTER US
FOR MILLENIUM AS YOU KNOW
THE TIME IS NOW TO LOOK AFTER HER
WE ALL MUST MAKE THIS SO,

NO MORE PLASTIC THROW AWAYS
NO MORE PLASTIC TRASH
THESE STEPS WON'T BE EASY
IN FACT THEY WILL BE QUITE HARSH,

BUT IF WE'RE VERY CAREFUL
CUT DOWN ON THIS AND THAT
WE BEQUETH THIS WORLD TO OUR CHILDREN
BE SURE WE LEAVE IT INTACT,

THINK OF THE ENVIROMENT
IN EVERYTHING WE DO
WE MUST MAKE SURE IN THE FUTURE
THAT THE SKY WILL STILL BE BLUE,

THE BEES THEY ARE A HUMMING
A SONG THEY SING TO ME
THE WORLD THEY SAY IS DIEING
THE TIME IS OVER FOR GLEE

BY CHOW MARTIN

LIFE AS A SOUND

WHAT WOULD LIFE BE LIKE
IF I WERE JUST A SOUND
I WOULD BE INFRONT AND BEHIND
I WOULD BE ALL AROUND,

I'D EXIST IN VIBRATION
CIRCULATING IN THE AIR
YOU CANNOT SEE ME
BUT I AM ALWAYS THERE,

WHEN YOU DO MOVE
I WOULD BE THERE
IN YOUR SQUEEKY DOORS
OR IN YOUR ROCKING CHAIR,

IN THE MOVING CARS
OR EVEN A MOVING TRAIN
YJE SOUND OF WALKING
OR THE RUMBLE OF A PLANE,

I COULD BE A WHISTLE
SO LOW AND SO SWEET
IN THE ROARING SEA
OR IN A BIRDS TWEET

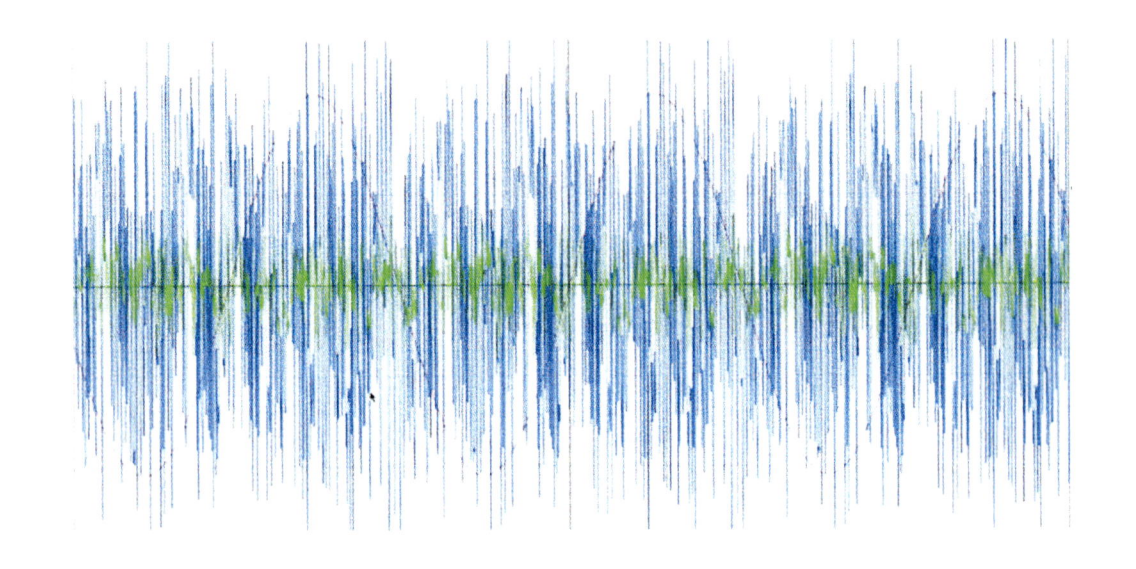

BY CATHIE MARTIN

THE MIRACULOUS STAIRCASE

IN THE LORETTO CHAPEL
NEW MEXICO, SANTA FE
THIS WAS TO BE A GIRLS SCHOOL
IN THE YEAR EIGHTEEN SEVENTY THREE,
TO GET UP TO THE TOP
THERE WAS NOTHING THERE
THE NUNS WANTED A STAIRCASE
THE LORD DID HEAR,
A SPIRAL STAIRCASE
DID GO ON SHOW
THE WOOD IS LIKE NO OTHER
NO-ONE DOTH KNOW,
THERE WAS NO GLUE OR NAILS USED
JUST WOODEN PEGS, NO SEAMS
NO CENTRAL COLUMN
WITH NO SUPPORTING BEAMS,
THIS TWENTY FOOT STAIRCASE
WITH THIRTY THREE STEPS SO HIGH
THE HELIX SHAPED SPIRAL STAIRCASE
THE NUNS WONDERED HOW WITH A SIGH
THIRTY THREE STEPS IS IRONIC
JESUS LIVED THAT LONG ON EARTH
THIRTY THREE YEARS THAT PASSED
UNTIL JESUSs' DEATH

BY CATHIE MARTIN

OTTO

I AM SIX YEAR OLD
 A FRENCH BULLDOG AM I
  I AM TENACIOUS, COURAGEOUS, TENDER
   SO LOVING I CAN MAKE YOU CRY,
     WHEN BORN MYSELF AND THE OTHERS
      WE WERE PUT IN A BOX
       WE WERE HAPPY PUPPIES
        I WAS ONE OF SIX ,
         THIS LOVELY LADY FRAUKE
          CAME INTO MY LIFE
            SHE'D TAKE ME LOVELY WALKS
             BY THE LOOSESTRIFE,
              RUNNING THROUGH THE SWARD
              THE AWNS, THE GRASSY GREEN
              HAVING SO MUCH FUN
              IT'S LIKE IN HEAVEN....YOU KNOW WHAT I MEAN,
                WE WOULD PLAY GAMES

                HAPPY I WOULD BE
                SO VERY VERY HAPPY THAT
                YOU ARE CLOSE TO ME,

SIX WONDERFUL YEARS
 THAT I HAVE WITH DOUGLAS AND YOU
   LOVING EVERY MINUTE
    ENJOYING THE THINGS WE DO,
                 I DON'T WANT NOTHING TO PART US MUM
                  COS I DO LOVE YOU SO
                   I CRY WHEN YOU GO AWAY SOMEWHERE
                   BECAUSE WITH YOU I CAN'T GO,
                    I BROUGHT LAUGHTER INTO YOUR LIFE
                     MAYBE A WEE SQUABBLE TOO
                      BUT ALL THAT GETS FORGOTTEN MUM
                       WHEN MY PUPPY DOG EYES LOOK AT YOU,

cntd..

I MISS MY KIN AND FRIENDS
   THAT I ONCE KNEW
      BUT I'VE A HAPPY LOVING LIFE
     WITH ME STAYING WITH YOU,
        I WILL CUDDLE UP AT NIGHT
           YOU KEEP ME WARM WITH YOU
            ALL CUDDLES AND KISSES
              SO LOVINGLY GIVEN TO ME TOO,
           ALL THE JOURNEY IN MY LIFE
              THE LOVING TIMES WITH SOME FEARS
            I'M HAPPY AND SO LUCKY
          THE MINUTES, DAYS AND YEARS,
              I'VE BEEN THROUGH A FEW STRIFES IN MY LIFE
          BUT I FEEL LOVE ALWAYS THERE
       I'VE PRINTED MY LIFE STORY BOOK
       WHICH IS SHOWN HERE, barcode 9783981789096 AVAILABLE @ AMAZON.COM,

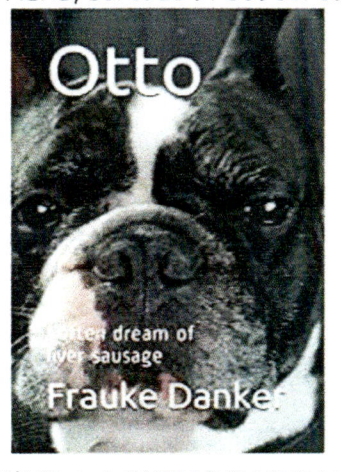

            I'VE A LOVING FAMILY
          ALL I FEEL IS AMOUR (LIEBE)
            I GET SPOILT EVERYDAY
            I COULDN'T ASK FOR MORE

BY OTTO UND FRAUKE DANKER

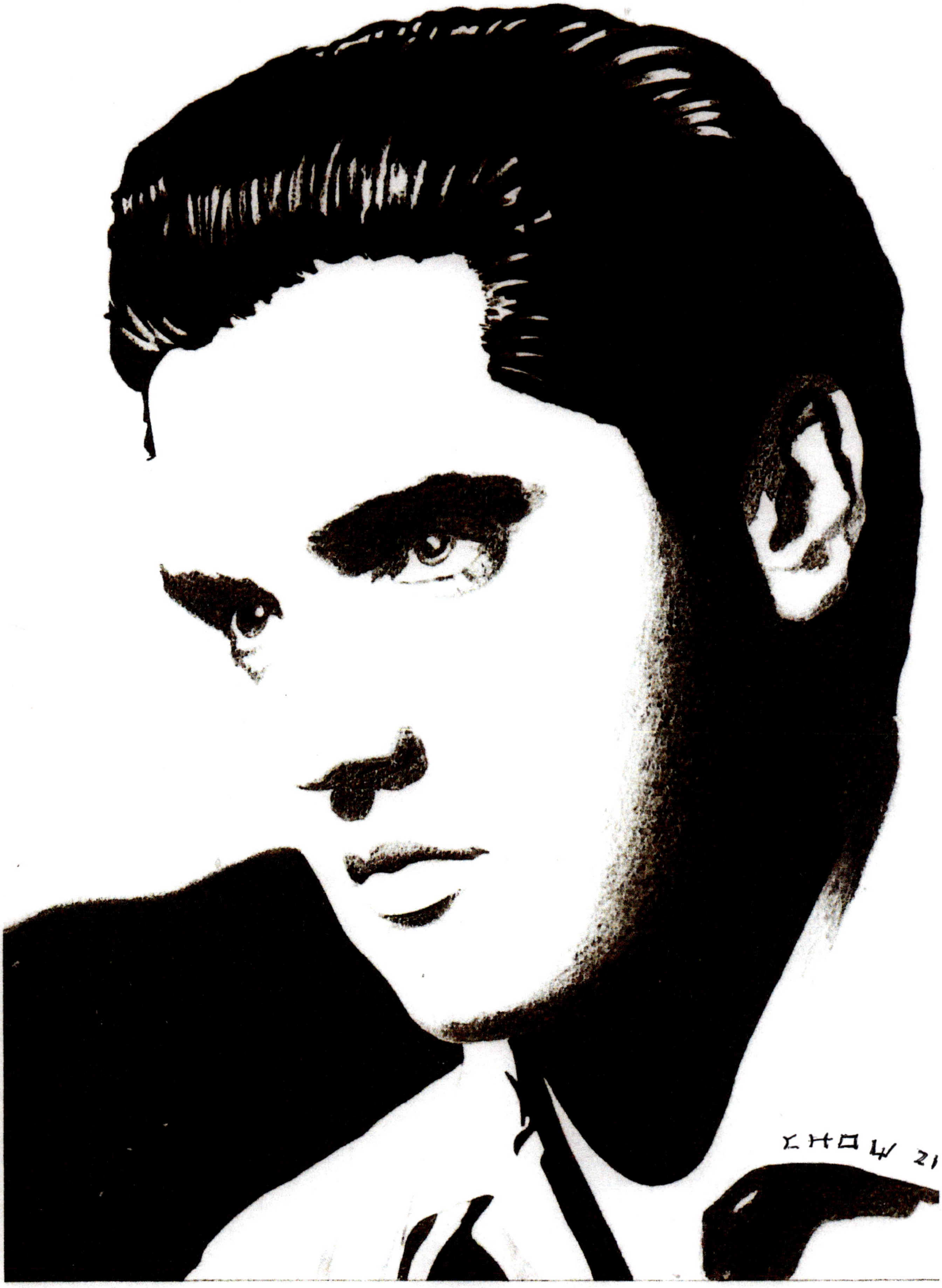
CHOW 21

A TRIBUTE TO **ELVIS PRESLEY**
1935-1977

MY DADDY WAS JAILED FOR HE DID DO WRONG
WE WERE A FAMILY POOR
AS I GREW UP AS A CHILD
I'D WORK HARD AND BE A DOER,
AT THE AGE OF FOUR I MADE A PROMISE
I SAID IT TO DAD AND MUM
I'D LOOK AFTER THEM AND BUY CADILLACS
IT WAS A PROMISE THAT WOULD GET DONE,
GOING TO SCHOOL FOR ME
WASN'T REALLY MUCH FUN
I'D GET TEASED AND BULLIED
I WAS A LONER A SHY ONE,
I'D CARRY AN ITTY BITTY GUITAR AROUND WITH ME
THAT'S WERE IT DID BELONG
I'D GO TO CHURCH AND 'CHARLIE'S RECORD SHOP
I DID LEARN TO SING SONG,
AT AGE OF TEN I SANG A SONG
ABOUT A DOG CALLED 'OLD SHEP'
IT WAS MY FIRST PUBLIC APPEARANCE
WAS I SHY? HELL YEP,
AT EIGHTEEN I WENT TO SUN RECORD LABELS
I RECORDED MY FIRST SONG
IT WAS CALLED 'MY HAPPINESS'
IT WAS A GIFT FOR MY MOM,
I HAD TO GO TO THE ARMY
AND DO MY JOB THERE
BUT WHEN I CAME OUT
I GOT A DIFFERENT CAREER,

I GOT INTO THE MOVIES
I WOULD ACT, DANCE AND SING
THE CHOREOGRAPHY WAS EASY
IT WAS A FUN TO DO THING,
I DID CAUSE MANY A TEAR
I MADE THEM FALL
BUT PEOPLE WERE THE HAPPIEST
THE HAPPIEST ONES OF ALL,
MOVING MY BODY
WHICH WAS AGAINST THE RULE
PEOPLE WOULD GO CRAZY
THEY THOUGHT IT SO COOL,
SLICK BLACK HAIR
MANY SUITS I DID CHOOSE
PLAYING ALONG WITH THIS GAME
I DID WIN.. I DID LOOSE,
I WENT FROM RAGS TO RICHES
CHANGES CAME TO MY LIFE

I MET A LOT OF PEOPLE
I EVEN TOOK A A WIFE,
DOING WHAT CAME UPON ME
I SANG MY LIFE AWAY
THEN THE LORD CAME A CALLING
SO NO MORE COULD I STAY,
MY MEMORIES ARE WITH YOU
I'VE LOVED YOU ALL FROM THE START
KEEP THINKING OF ME
KEEP MY SONGS IN YOUR HEART

BY CATHIE MARTIN

SOLDIER BOY

YOU FIGHT FOR YOUR COUNTRY
THE YOUNG SOLDIER BOY YOU ARE
TREADING HOPE AND GLORY
FOLLOW THAT BRIGHT STAR,
ALL THE PEOPLE WITH COURAGE
COUNTRIES FIGHT FOR FAME
THIS IS ALL TOO SERIOUS
DON'T LOOK AT IT AS A GAME,
OVER THE LAND THERE ARE MANY
THAT ARE TOLD WHAT TO DO
THEY DO THE ULTIMATE DUTY
THEY ARE FIGHTING FOR YOU,
THE PRINCIPLES AND CREEDS
THE MIGHTY AND THE STRONG
FIGHTING FOR THE GOOD
YOU CARRY YOUR HOPES ALONG,
IS IT WAR OR PEACE
WHAT SIDE DO YOU CHOOSE
THERE CAN BE AN UNDERSTANDING
BATTLES THAT WIN AND LOSE,
HOLD YOUR HEAD HIGH SOLDIERS
YOU FIGHT WITHOUT FEAR
BUT WHEN THE WAR IS OVER
ALL THE HEARTACHES THAT ARE THERE

BY CATHIE MARTIN

THE DREAM WEAVER

FULLFILL THE DREAMS
LET THE HEART BE ALIVE
THE WILLING TO WANT
THE NEED TO OVERLOVE,
THE VISION OF PERSONS
BE IT FICTION OR REAL
THE WARMTH OVER COMING
THE DREAMS DO I FEEL,

ART BY ROMEO TANGHAL Sr

COMPASSION, THE TIMELESSNESS
THOUGHTS OF THE UNKNOWN
LAYING ALONE IN THE DARK
HOT TEMPERATURE AND A MOAN,
BEAUTY IS ABOUND
LOVELINESS, A BELIEVER
AT NIGHT IN A WORLD
OF THE DREAM WEAVER

POEM BY CATHIE MARTIN

DISABILITY

I AM DISABLED
BUT THERE'S WORSE OFF THAN ME
I HAVE MY OWN MIND
I AM NOT SICK
I AM NOT NEEDY
MY EYES ARE NOT BLIND,
  I CAN DO A LITTLE
  I TRY TO HELP
  I WILL THINK OF OTHERS
  WE ALL HAVE A FRIEND
  IN OUR MOTHER AND FATHER
  OR IN OUR SISTERS AND BROTHERS,
I SMILE AT PEOPLE
TO CHEER THEM UP
A NICE THING TO DO
I SHAKE HANDS
WHEN THE FRIENDS I MEET
I SAY 'HI, HELLO TO YOU'
  I'M NOT AN ALIEN
  A NORMAL HUMAN AM I
  I'M MADE OF BLOOD AND BONES TOO
  SEE ME AS A PERSON
  NOT JUST MY DISABILITY
  I HAVE A LIFE JUST LIKE YOU DO

BY CATHIE AND CHOW MARTIN

WORDS

I MAY BE DEAF
BUT DUMB I'M NOT
I LEARNED A SIGN LANGUAGE
IT'S HOW I TALK,
I USE MY HANDS
MY LIPS SOMETIMES TOO
THIS IS HOW I COMMUNICATE
MY FEELINGS TO YOU,
IF YOU SEE ME
DON'T STOP AND STARE
YOU'D HURT MY FEELINGS
TO MUCH TO BARE,
BUT FOR THE GRACE OF GOD
YOU COULD HAVE BEEN THIS WAY TOO
LIVING IN A DIFFERENT WORLD
NO SOUNDS THAT ARE NEW,
WE USE OUR EYES
FOR HEAR WE CANNOT
WE LIP READ DAILY
FOR THIS IS OUR LOT

by mr chow martin

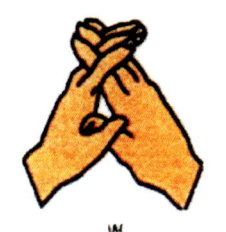

W O R D S

BY CHOW MARTIN

SILENT WAR (coronavirus)

WAR'S NOT WHAT YOU IMAGINE
A SILENT KILLER IT CAN BE
THERE IS LEFT A DEVASTATION
MUCH MORE THAN YOU CAN SEE,
THOUGHTS AND EMOTIONS
THE FUTURE IS FULL OF REGRET
IMPOSSIBLE TO HIDE FEELINGS
THIS FIGHT IS A THREAT,
THE WORLDS NOT WHAT YOU KNOW IT
IT'S NOT HOW IT USED TO BE
BUT FREEDOM IS NO LONGER
WE'RE CAUGHT, YOU AND ME,
THIS KILLER IS A DANGER
NO MORE JOY AND JUBILEE
THE POISON OF THE SILENT KILLER
WE ARE NO MORE FREE,
WE GO FIGHTING ONWARDS
WITH HOPE IN OUR HEART
BUT THIS SILENT KILLER
WILL KEEPS US ALL APART

THE SILENT KILLER

BY CATHIE MARTIN

VICTIM

MY LIFE AS A VICTIM IS PAINFUL I SAY
MY LIFE AS A VICTIM IS HELL EVERY DAY

I'M BULLIED, I'M WEAK, I'M NOT WORTH A THING
I'D LOVE TO BE HAPPY, LIKE A BIRD I WOULD SING

I'M BULLIED AT SCHOOL, I'M BULLIED AT HOME,
I SEEM TO BE BULLIED WHERE EVER I ROAM

I'VE GOT TO GET STRONG FOR ALL THE WORLD TO SEE
I'VE GOT TO GET STRONG BE ALL THAT I CAN BE

STRONG IN THE MIND AND THE BODY I'LL BECOME
NO ONE WILL PICK ON ME THEN...I'LL BE SOMEONE

BY CHOW MARTIN

ALIENS

THEY COME FROM A PLANET
THAT IS FAR AWAY
THEY LIVE THEIR LIVES
IN A DIFFERENT WAY

IN THE DARKEST HOUR
FROM ANOTHER WORLD THEY CAME
WITH A DIFFERENT APPEARANCE
THEY ARE NOT THE SAME

THE LIGHT FROM THEIR SHIP
SHONE DOWN ON MY FACE
COMING DOWN TO INVESTIGATE
THE HUMAN RACE

LARGE HEADS, BIG EYES
NO NOSES TO SMELL
LONG FINGERS AND TOES
LONG BODIES AS WELL

THEY TAKE YOU TO THEIR CRAFT
THEY PROBE AND THEY TOUCH
THE EXPERIMENTS THEY DO
HURT YOU SO MUCH

NO ONE BELIEVES YOU
WHEN THEY LET YOU GO
THEY'LL COME BACK FOR YOU AGAIN
AND YOU CAN'T SAY NO

BY CHOW MARTIN

QUEEN OF FANTASY

THROUGH THE YEARS AND TEARS
ALL THE LOVE AND FRIENDSHIP COMBINED
THE WARMING LIPS, THE KISSES TRUE
THE HOLDING, ALL THE FEELINGS TWINED,
IN A WORLD OF FANTASY
QUEEN OF THOUGHT AM I
BUILDING UP OF THE EMOTIONS
IS IT HAPPINESS I FEEL... I WANT TO CRY,
THE SWEETNESS, THE BLISS
THE BEATING HEART GROWS
THE MASK OF LIVING AND LEARNING
THE WANTING, IT SHOWS,

ART BY ROMEO TANGHAL Sr

THE DOORS HAVE ALL OPENED
A GUIDANCE, THE DIRECTION OF QUALITY TRUE
THE SWIRLING OF THOUGHTS
THE POWER OF DREAMING TO DO,
APPROACHING UPON THE BURSTS OF ENLIGHTENMENT
THE PURPOSE OF MUST, WANT, NEED OR TO GIVE
TO DREAM, TO LOVE THE AWAKENING OF BEING
I'M THE QUEEN OF FANTASY IN YOUR MIND I DO LIVE

poem by cathie martin

WALKING TOGETHER

WALKING DOWN ELLEN'S GLEN
WITH THE ONE I LOVE
THE SUN IS SHINING
THE BIRDS ARE UP ABOVE,
IT IS A LOVELY DAY
TO SHARE WITH YOU
SO HAPPY AND CAREFREE
SO PEACEFUL TOO,
JUST STROLLING ALONG
ARM IN ARM TOGETHER WE BE
NO SHADOWS IN THE SKY
WHAT LOVELY COMPANY,
ENJOYING THE TIME
WE HAVE TOGETHER
WE WILL REMEMBER THIS DAY ALWAYS
FOREVER AND EVER

TRIBUTE TO MY FATHER MR PETR O'DAY AND MOTHER MOLLIE O'DAY
BY CATHIE MARTIN

ELLENS GLEN, GILMERTON EDINBURGH

IF IT'S IN THE PAPERS !!

"IF IT'S IN THE PAPERS, THE MEDIA
IT MUST ALWAYS BE TRUE
COS IT'S IMPORTANT IMFORMATION
FOR EVERYONE TO READ NOT JUST A FEW,
THERE'S AN AMAZING STORY CATHIE
THAT DOGS COULD RULE THE WORLD
WE WILL ALL BE TOGETHER
IN THE MEADOWS, PLAINS LIFE WILL BE UNRUFFLED,
I BELIEVE IT COULD BE TRUE
IT'S OUR IMPORTANCE OF BEING
NOT JUST A PROBABILITY
IT WILL BE FOR THE SEEING,"

*"ha ha, OKAY OTTO IF YOU SEE THAT THERE
MIND READ THE SMALL PRINT THAT'S THERE IN THE SQUARE
IT SAYS 'WATCH OUT WORLD BE PREPARED BE AWARE,
ROBOTS WILL TAKE OVER OUR MOTHER EARTH
THERE'S GONNA BE A NEW BIRTH
EVERYONE WILL KNOW THEIR SELF WORTH"*

"BUT CATHIE LOOK AT THE CENTREFOLD
THE PICTURE LOOKS REAL
NOW WHAT DO YOU SAY
HOW SILLY DO YOU FEEL?"

COLONEL OTTO

YOU HUMANS WILL DO OUR BID
BE AT OUR BECK AND CALL
WE SHALL OVER POWER
BE THE MIGHTIEST OF ALL"

cntd..

"JA OTTO YES YOU'LL GOVEN LAND AND SEA
BUT WHAT ABOUT LOVE THAT'S FREE
NO CRUELTY NO OPPRESSION TO BE,
CAUGHT IN OUR OWN PRISON
AN INSANITY, A REASON
EVERY YEAR, EVERY SEASON,
RESPONSIBILITIES TO SHARE
FOR EVERYONE OUT THERE
ALL TO DO THIS MUST PREPARE,"

"AS SOON AS WE GOVERN
("SOWIE SOBALD WIR REGIEREN)
I WILL LET YOU ALL KNOW
BUT FORGET THE PAPERS
LET'S JUST GO HOME,
MY DINNER IS AWAITING
I FEEL A BIT SADDENED
YOU'LL FEED ME YOU WILL
DO YOU SEE WHAT JUST HAPPENED"

BY OTTO DANKER UND CATHIE MARTIN

WHO REMEMBERS WHEN YESTERDAY WAS JUST DOWN THE ROAD TO THE LEFT

FILLED WITH DELIGHT AND DREAMS
YOU ASK YOURSELF WHAT IS THE WAY
TAKING YOU BACK TO THE MEMORY
DOWN THE ROAD JUST LIKE YESTERDAY,
RECALL THE GOOD THE MOMENTS OF AWE
MISTAKES, BLUNDERS THAT ARE HEFT
TRAVEL WHICH WAY TO ARRIVE
YESTERDAY DOWN THE ROAD TO THE LEFT,
THIS LONG EMPTY ROUTE
IS YOUR LIFE LIKE IN A WEFT
A JOURNEY THAT LASTS FOREVER, NO END
JUST LIKE YESTERDAY DOWN THE ROAD TO THE LEFT

BY CATHIE MARTIN

CONAN

BORN ON THE BATTLEFIELD
MY MOTHER DIED JUST AFTER MY BIRTH
I WAS BORN AS A CIMMERIAN
AND I SWEAR TO RULE THIS EARTH

A SKILLED BLACKSMITH IS MY FATHER
CORIN IS HIS NAME
CHIEF OF THE BARBARIAN TRIBE
MASTER SWORDSMAN IS HIS FAME

MY FATHER HAD THE DAUNTING TASK
OF RAISING THIS SAVAGE CHILD
I'M A KILLER THAT'S MATURED
I'M SO SMART AND WILD

I WAS TAUGHT THE MEANING OF THE SWORD
I MUST TEMPER THIS HOT BURNING BLADE
TO FIGHT ALL MY ENEMIES
I STAND TALL, I AM NOT AFRAID

ON MY FIFTEENTH BIRTHDAY
I HAD TO SLAY WOLVES FOR THEIR KILL
I WAS SEDUCED AT THIS YOUNG AGE
IT MADE ME A MAN WITH STRONG WILL

I'M KNOWN AS A THEIF AND A SLAYER
I'VE GOT A GIGANTIC MIRTH
I'VE BLACK HAIR AND SULLEN EYES
I TREAD THE JEWLLED THRONES OF THE EARTH

I HAVE THE STRENGTH OF MANY MEN
I'M A PHYSICAL POWERFUL MAN
I'M MUSCULAR WITH MENTAL TOUGHNESS
MY SURVIVAL INSTINCTS SUPERHUMAN

I AM COMMANDER AND LEADER
I SHALL CRUSH MY ENIMIES DOWN
I FEAR ALL UNKNOWN GODS
MY DEITY IS CROM

POEM BY CATHIE MARTIN CONAN CREATED BY ROBERT E HOWARD

REMNANTS

Your creative life's remnants lie set about me
Comforting abscence in careful placement
Preserving fullness of memory
Love's token
Blessing
Inclusion for the journey
Providing warmth in kind reminder
Provoking thought of remnants of my own.

BY Rosemarie Ashton

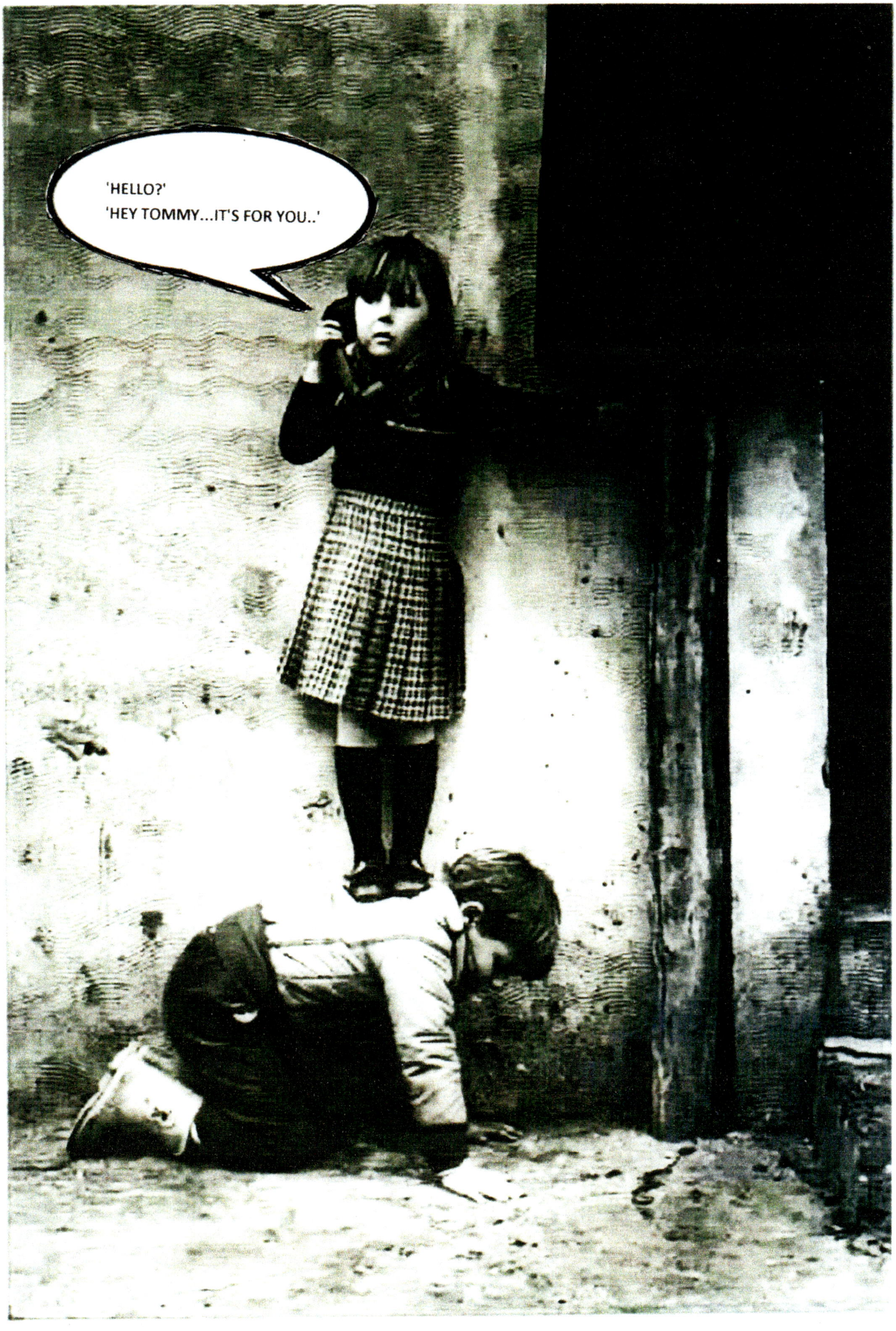
'HELLO?'
'HEY TOMMY...IT'S FOR YOU..'

THE MEANING OF LIFE

THERE IS NO DEFINITION IN LIFE
EACH DAY IS NEVER THE SAME
FOR EVERY LIVING SOUL
NO MATTER WHAT YOUR NAME
LIFE IS A CLICK OF A CAMERA
YOU FOCUS ON WHAT YOU SEE
YOU CAPTURE THE GOOD AND BAD
YOU CAPTURE WHAT IS TO BE
LIFE IS LIKE A BOOK
EACH PAGE IS A PART OF YOU
IT IS LIKE A PLAY
THE ACTING YOU HAVE TO DO
LEAVES WILL FALL FROM A TREE
SOME LEAVES WILL NOT
BUILT UP RAGE CAN CAUSE WARS
WHEN IT GETS RAGING HOT
AFTER YOU'VE EXPERIENCED STRIFE
SOLITUDE DOES RELEASE
THE MOMENTS OF REALITY
THEN YOU'LL FEEL THE PEACE

IS THERE A POINT IN LIFE
NOT KNOWING WHEN IT WILL END
YOU GO THROUGH EVERY MOMENT
NONE THE WISER YOU JUST PRETEND
WHATEVER YOU WANT IT TO BE
IS THE MEANING OF LIFE
QUIET, HAPPY LIVING
OR THE WARS THAT ARE RIFE

BY CHOW AND CATHIE MARTIN

LIFES' QUESTION

WILL THE ANGELS COME AND FETCH ME
WHEN IT'S TIME FOR ME TO GO?
WILL THE LORD REACH OUT AND TOUCH ME?
WILL I EVER REALLY KNOW?
WILL THERE BE A NEW TOMORROW?
SHALL I FIND A BRAND NEW DAY?
WILL I UNDERSTAND LIFE'S MEANING?
OR JUST SIMPLY PASS AWAY?

BY ROSEMARIE ASHTON

THE BEAUTY OF LOVE

ART BY ROMEO TANGHAL Sr

Embrace me in your arms
Hot love let me feel
I am a woman
I am wanting, I am real,
Emotions out pouring
The need of you I pleed
Hold me tight my love
Forever in you I need,
With my insecurities and imperfections
I reveal myself to you
I open my heart and my soul
In love the togetherness of two,
I am the beauty
In the night , in the day
The warmth of your body
Forever with me will stay

POEM BY CATHIE MARTIN

HUDSON RIVER KINGSTON NEW YORK USA

THE COUNTY COURTHOUSE SOMERSET NEW JERSEY USA

SOMERSET COUNTY COURT HOUSE GREEN

The Somerset County Court House, constructed in 1909, is a fine example of Beaux-Arts Classicism. It was designed by the firm of Carère, Tracy and Swartwout. James Reilly Gordon was one of America's greatest courthouse architects, who also designed the Arizona State Capitol. The Court House was the location of the Hauptmann Hall Mills murder trial in 1926.

The First Reformed Church, constructed in 1897, is a free interpretation of an English Gothic church. It was designed by William Appleton Potter renowned for his architecture on the Princeton University campus. The Lord Memorial Fountain, erected in 1910, was designed by John Russell Pope, designer of the Jefferson Memorial, and sculpted by John Boyle and Thomas Trotesera.

TEMPLE OF JERUSALEM

RUINS OF LILLESHALL ABBEY SHROPSHIRE ENGLAND

CALTON HILL EDINBURGH

CRAMOND CAUSEWAY SCOTLAND

RHONNDA VALLEY WALES

MINING MUSEUM NEWTONGRANGE

CALATRAVAS, TWISTING SKYSCRAPER SWEDEN

HOTEL GURU HANOVER GERMANY

SNOW WHITE'S COTTAGE OLALLA WASHINGTON

WARM LOVE

BEFORE I DO SLEEP AT NIGHT
MY MIND THINKS OF YOU
ALL OF THESE PRECIOUS MOMENTS
THAT I CAN SEND MY LOVE TOO,
YOU MIGHT BE ONLY ONE
BUT THE WORLD YOU ARE TO ME
A WARM HUG I FEEL IN MY HEART
THAT NO-ONE ELSE CAN SEE,
A KISS UPON MY LIPS
NOT ONLY IN MY DREAM
MY EYES THEY FILL WITH TEARS
DOWN MY CHEEKS THEY DO STREAM,
IS THERE A REASON FOR
ALL MY LOVE FOR YOU
I CAN'T TELL OR SHOW YOU
I JUST KNOW THAT IT IS TRUE

BY CATHIE MARTIN

I LAUGHED AND LAUGHED!

EVERYDAY I GET A WASH
MAKE MY FACE AND BODY CLEAN
I'M IN THE WATER FOR A WHILE
AT LEAST THAT'S THE WAY IT DOES SEEM,
I'LL SPLASH ABOUT IN THE WATER
PLAY WITH MY TOYS AS WELL
I DO GET AWFULLY SOAPY
WHICH MAKES A LOVELY SMELL,
MAKING BUBBLES AN HAVING FUN
I'LL LAUGH AND LAUGH AND GIGGLE
SPLASHING IN THE WATER
I'LL SQUIGGLE AND JIGGLE
I'LL SEE MY LITTLE WINKLE
WHEN I'M SITTING IN THE BATH
IT'S NOT GOT A BEND LIKE CLINTONS
BUT IT MAKES ME LAUGH AND LAUGH,
I'LL GROW UP SOMEDAY
AND MY WINKLE TOO
YOU SEE I'M JUST A WEE LAD
OCH! I'M ONLY TWO

BY CATHIE MARTIN

BULLY

I CAUGHT MY BROTHER KISSING THE GIRL ACROSS THE STREET

I TEASED HIM THAT I WAS GOING TO TELL DAD

HER NAME WAS BARBARA VANDEVENDER AND SHE SAID TO ME "Toni Baloney what makes you so fat, the head of a chicken the tail of a rat"

I said "Barbara what makes you so cruel is your mom a witch does she feed you gruel, I'm looking at you and i shake my head gosh almighty what have your parents made?, my blood boils when i see your face why are you on this planet here with the human race, across the street you live we all see you there jack likes you i think your a scare, a nasty girl i hope you get paid back with your face of a blobfish and the body of a yak"

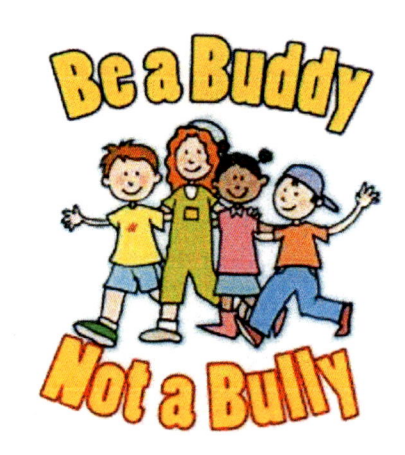

BY TONI BEEDLE

STUPIDITY

EVERYONE HAS A POINT OF IGNORANCE
WE ARE ALL BORN THAT WAY
IGNORANT OF THE KNOW WHAT AND HOW
BUT YOUR LESS IGNORANT DAY BY DAY,
JUST THE ABSENCE OF KNOWLEDGE
YOUR NOT DAFT OR DUMB
IN OUR MIND IS AN EMPTY SPACE
EASIER FOR OTHERS TO FILL THAN SOME,
UNDERESTIMATING PEOPLES WORTH
MISUNDERESTIMATING THEIR SITUATION
YOUR BEING OF PRIDE AND WISDOM
IS A KNOW HOW OF ELATION

BY CATHIE MARTIN

THE LIGHTHOUSE

I'M THE TALL LIGHTHOUSE
STANDING ALL ALONE
I'M THERE IN ALL WEATHERS
THEY CHILL ME TO THE BONE
I STAND IN THE DARK
I STAND IN THE LIGHT
I STAND IN THE DAY
I STAND IN THE NIGHT
THE CREAKING SOUNDS
AS I TURN MY HEAD
I STAND TO ATTENTION
NEVER LAY DOWN IN BED
I'M KNOWN TO BE CALLED
THE ANGEL OF THE NIGHT
THE WISEST THING AT SEA
THAT KEEPS THINGS ALRIGHT
A FOG WILL APPEAR
SO THICK AND DENSE
A STORM WILL RAGE
SO WILD AND IMMENSE
I'LL WARN OF THE DANGERS THERE
I AM THE ALARM
BY SHINING MY LIGHT
I'LL PROTECT YOU FROM HARM

BY CATHIE MARTIN

SO POWERFUL

I AM SO POWERFUL
I AM THE SUN
NOTHING IS STRONGER
I AM NUMBER ONE,
I AM YOUR FATHER
I AM YOUR MOTHER
I AM ALL THINGS INBETWEEN
TO ME THERE IS NO OTHER,
I GIVE YOU LIFE
I GIVE YOU HOPE
I GIVE YOU WEATHER
YOU SOMETIMES CANNOT COPE,
I MAKE YOU STRONG
I MAKE YOU WEAK
YOUR LESS THAN ANTS
UNDER MY HEAVENLY FEET,
SO NEAR YOU GET CLOSER
OR GO AWAY IN A DISTANT
OF WHICH I'VE EXPERIENCED MANY
YOUR LIFE IS A FLEETING INSTANT,
I AM IMPORTANT
I WILL NEVER SHIFT
TO BE BLINDED BY MY BEAUTY
TO BEHOLD ME IS A GIFT

BY CHOW MARTIN

DON'T CRY FOR ME

WHEN I'M NOT HERE
WHEN I'M DEAD AND GONE
DON'T CRY FOR ME
YOUR LIFE STILL GOES ON,
DON'T STAND AT MY GRAVE
DON'T SHED ME A TEAR
REMEMBER MY DARLING
I WILL STILL BE HERE,
OUR HEARTS ARE TOGETHER
THEY WILL ALWAYS BE
REMEMBER THE HAPPY TIMES
DON'T CRY FOR ME,
WHISPERS OF MY NAME
IN ALL THE BIRDS YOU SEE
BE STRONG MY DARLING
DON'T CRY FOR ME,
WE WILL MEET AGAIN
IT MAY TAKE A WHILE
DON'T CRY FOR ME
BE HAPPY AND SMILE,
OUR TIME TOGETHER
YOU WILL REMEMBER THIS
LOOK UP TO THE HEAVENS
AND BLOW ME A KISS

BY CATHIE MARTIN

AGED AND IN LOVE

TO FIND WHO WOULD BE TO LOVE YOU
SEARCH FOR YEARS WE DON'T CARE
WE KNEW THERE WAS LOVE
OUR SOUL MATE WAS THERE,
WHEN MY LIFE WAS A VOID
YOU CAME INTO MY WORLD
THEN EVERYDAY FROM THEN ON
IT WAS COMPLETLY LOVE AND FURLED,
THERE WOULD BE TOUGH MOMENTS
BUT WE WOULD SEE THEM THROUGH
MY DARLING COMPANION
YOU LOVE ME AS MUCH AS I LOVE YOU,
FOREVER AND A DAY
WE CHERISH THE TIME
WHAT'S YOURS IS YOURS
AND WHAT'S YOURS IS MINE,
SHARE ALL WE HAVE
IT'S A JOURNEY OF LOVE THAT WILL BIDE
ALWAYS FOREVER MY DARLING
I WILL BE BY YOUR SIDE,
ALL OUR LOVING DAYS
NO MATTER HOW AGED WE BECOME
THE LOVE DOES GROW STRONGER
THERE WILL NEVER BE ANOTHER ONE,
OLD AND WRINKLED LIKE TIME ITSELF
OUR LIFE IS WORTH LIVING
THERE'S NO EXPIRY DATE ON LOVE
WE ARE LOVING AND FORGIVING,
WE CHERISH EVERY MOMENT
SO SPECIAL WITH YOU
WE LOVED EACH OTHER WHEN WE MET
LOVE THEN, LOVE NOW, LOVE ALWAYS WE DO

BY CATHIE MARTIN

I WANNA BE.....

I WISH I WAS
A BABY BEAR
CUDDLY AND LOVING
BUT GOING NOWHERE,
WITH TWO BUTTON EYES
AND A WEE BLACK NOSE
A HAPPY SMILE
THAT'S HOW IT GOES,
I'D BE BESIDE YOU
EVERY SINGLE DAY
HAVING LOTS OF FUN
AS WE DO PLAY,
KISSES AND CUDDLES FROM YOU
AS YOU HOLD ME TIGHT
I AM A LITTLE TEDDY BEAR
A CUDDLY TOY AT NIGHT

BY CATHIE MARTIN

POEMS FOR THE PEOPLE

MAKING THE READER FEEL SOMETHING
THE EXPRESSION OF WORDS TO READ
THE CONVENTIONAL WISDOM SHARED
SHALL BE ACCEPTED BY ALL INDEED,

THE ABILITY OF THOUGHT PROVOKING
THE INSPIRATION TO THE HIGHEST PINNACLE
SAYING WHAT NEEDS TO BE FELT
MAKES THE WORDS TO BE WINNABLE,

RECOGNISE THE ELEMENT OF PURPOSE
EXPERIENCE ALL THE EMOTIONS TOO
WHAT IS WRITTEN IS TO BE SAID
IN THE RHYMES FROM MYSELF TO YOU,

TO INTEPRET THE MEANINGS
ALL OPINIONS SHALL BE FAIR
POEMS FOR THE PEOPLE
THAT EVERYONE CAN SHARE

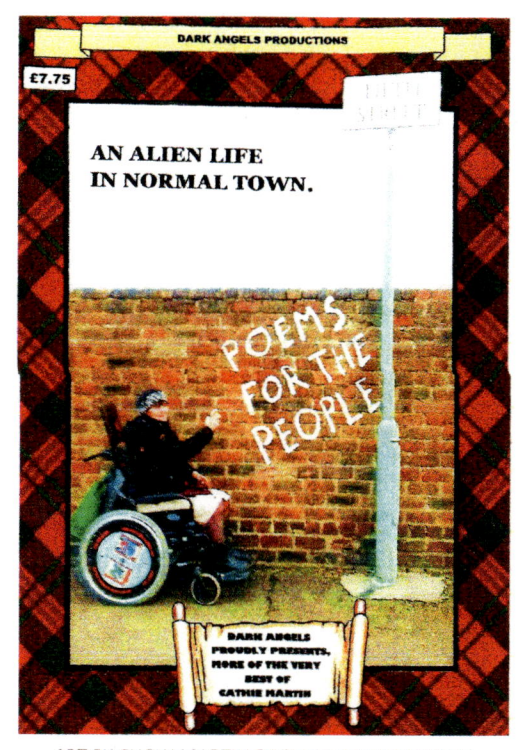

ART BY CHOW MARTIN POEM BY CATHIE MARTIN

ONE

Leave me in a ditch
Leave me to die
Bury me underground
Oh my, oh my...

Carve into my flesh
With a rusty knife
Eat my rotten brain
And taste my life

Flourish in my sorrow
Feel my dispair
Never let it out
It's only fair

by Rebecca Hedberg

DA DE DA DEE DA

I'LL BE PERFECT TOMORROW
OR SOMEDAY WHEN
YOU REMEMBER ME
AS I WAS THEN
AND HOW I COULD BE AGAIN
DA DE DA DEE DA

MY WAY IS NOW TO BE
THOUGH ALIVE IN THE MIND
A TRUTHFUL SOUL
SO WORTHY AND KIND
MY WORTHNESS YOU WILL FIND
DA DE DA DEE DA

BY BRIAN SMITH

DIFFERENCES

WE'RE ON A PATH IN LIFE
WITH AN UNEXPLAINED DIFFERENCE
A COURSE FOR ONE OR THE OTHER
WHICH IS WHATEVER OUR PREFERENCE,

EXTREMITIES DIFFICULT TO THE END
THE SAME FOR YOU AND I
EVERYONE IS AN EQUAL
WE LIVE, WE BREATH, WE DIE,

THE JOURNEY SHALL BREAK PEOPLE
A FRIENDSHIP HERE AND THERE
THOUGH YOUR HEART IS LONELY
DEEP DOWN WE ALL DO CARE,

WE DO OUR UPTMOST BEST
TO PLEASE IN OUR OWN WAY
THE DAYS, THE YEARS OF LIVING
ALWAYS THIS WAY WE'LL STAY

BY CATHIE MARTIN

TOILET ROLL

IT'S AN ESSENTIAL COMMODITY
THAT EVERYONE DOES NEED
NO-ONE LIKES TO MENTION IT
BUT OUR JOB DOES PROCEED,
IT'S ROUND IN SHAPE
CAN BE A LOVELY COLOUR
CAN BE SOFT AND GENTLE
FROM YOU WE'RE MUCH SMALLER,
USE IT FOR WIPING OR MOPING UP
TO BLOW YOUR NOSE ONCE OR TWICE
DAB AWAY THE WATER
IF YOUR EYES CRIES,
WE MIGHT SIT ON THE CISTERN
OR YOU HANG US ON THE WALL
WE WON'T SAY ANYTHING
ALTHOUGH WE SEE IT ALL,
WE ALL WAIT PATIENLY
WE ALL STAY BY
YOU'LL FINISH YOUR CHORE
THEN GIVE A HAPPY SIGH,
OUR RESPONSIBILITY
IS TO KEEP THINGS CLEAN
THE AROMA MAY BE PUNGENT
YOU KNOW WHAT I MEAN,
WE CAN WAIT FOR A LONG TIME
NO COMPANY FOR US
THEN PEOPLE APPEAR
IN MAYBE A RUSH,
STAYING HERE IN EVERY WEATHER
BE IT HOT OR COLD
WE HELP OUT EVERYONE
FROM THE YOUNG TO THE OLD,
WHEN OUR ROLL IS EMPTY
OUR JOB IS DONE
YOU'LL GO AND REPLACE US
WITH A NICE SOFT NEW ONE

BY CATHIE MARTIN

A LOADED DICE

Deep within
Beyond time and place
Transcending energy and
form
Waves prance to rhythms of
yesterday and tomorrow

Alone
Paired
Travelling
In a standstill
Charting an intricate course
of decisive uncertainty

Life dances death in reticent
abandon
Long gone Gods in
ambitious despair
Peace dies in the raging still
of battle
A universe sheds its own
fabric of being

Deep within
Beyond eyes and face
Transcending villainy and
scorn
Telitale designs at the
crossroads of here and now
Cast a loaded dice in
suspicious anxiety

BY MICHAEL NETZER

HELL!

ART BY MR CHOW MARTIN

THE SCREAMING THE PLEADING
THIS DREADFUL HELL
WERE EVIL BODIES ARE
WHERE THE DEMONS DWELL,
THE HEARTS AND SOULS CRUSHED
NO CONSCIOUS OF LIVING
AMONG ALL THE DEAD
THERE IS ANOTHER BEING,
THE RIVER OF DEATH
PEOPLE WILL PAY FOR THEIR SIN
YOU CAN PRAY TO GOD
BUT THE DEVIL SHALL WIN

BY CHOW MARTIN

> WHY YES, THERE IS A GUY STANDING NEXT TO ME WHO LOOKS LIKE A COMPLETE IDIOT. DO YOU WISH TO SPEAK TO HIM?

> HEY SUGAR LIPS!....IT'S FOR YOU!

BY MR CHOW MARTIN

GLOBAL

ART BY MR CHOW MARTIN

ABOUT THE GLOBAL WARMING
DO YOU KNOW WHAT IT MEANS
EVERYWHERE AROUND
IS BURSTING AT THE SEAMS
THE ICE CAPS ARE MELTING AWAY
THE SEA LEVELS WILL ALL RISE
OUR WORLD WILL BE DIFFERENT
THE SPECIES OF EVERYTHING DIES
THE USE OF FOSSIL FUEL
VOLCANIC ERUPTION
WE ARE ALL TO BLAME
WE HAVE DIFFERENT PERCEPTION
THE METHANE GASSES
THE TEMPERATURE KEEPS RISING
THE DROUGHT IN THE WORLD
SLOWLY OUR LIVES ARE ALL PASSING
GOODBYE TO THIS WORLD
WE REALLY WIPED IT OUT OURSELVES
MAYBE A NEW WORLD WILL COME
YOU WON'T SEE IT YOURSELVES

A GOOD MAN'S HARD TO FIND
SO WHY NOT MAKE ONE YOURSELF

YOU THINK ABOUT HAVING A MAN IN YOUR LIFE
BUT WHO WOULD YOU FIND
WOULD IT BE SOMEONE WITH A HEALTHY BODY
MOST OF ALL AN INTELLIGENT MIND,
FEED HIM BRAINY FOOD
AND YOU CAN WALK AND TALK TO HIM
HE WON'T GROW A BEARD OR MOUSTACHE
HE WON'T GET FAT HE'LL ALWAYS STAY SLIM,

CUDDLE UP TO HIM NIGHTLY
TELL HIM A JOKE OR TWO
HE WOULD LAUGH AWAY QUIETLY
AND BE DEEPLY IN LOVE WITH YOU,
HE'D BE BY YOUR SIDE FOR ALWAYS
EVERY MINUTE OF THE DAY
YOU CAN MAKE THIS GOOD MAN PERFECT
YOU CAN MAKE HIM IN YOUR WAY

BY CATHIE AND CHOW MARTIN

ANIMAL FONDNESS

THE ANIMALS LIKE TO HAVE FUN
ANIMALS LIKE TO PLAY
LOVE ALL THE CREATURES
BE KIND WITH WHAT YOU SAY,
ANIMALS LIKE A CUDDLE
MAYBE A PAT ON THE BACK
THEY WILL BE FRIENDLY
WITH NO NEED FOR ATTACK,
IN THEIR OWN KIND OF WAY
THE RECIPROCATION THEY WILL DO
FRIENDLINESS AND LOVING
THEY WILL SHOW IT TO YOU,

BE FRIENDLY WITH A TWEETY BIRD
A PUPPY DOG OR CAT
WINTER ANIMALS OR SUMMER ANIMALS
OR MAYBE A LOVELY WEE BAT,
CUTENESS, ADORATION
LOVELY COLOURS AS WELL
SMARTNESS SO CLEVER
THEY CAN PUT YOU IN A SPELL,
BE FRIENDLY WITH ALL ANIMALS
THEY CAN BE SMALL OR BIG
FRIENDLINESS IS WELCOME BY ALL
EVEN THIS DARLING WEE PIG

by cathie and chow martin

THE HORROR

WHEN YOUR IN THE HOUSE
SITTING ALL ALONE
IN THE DARK AND QUIET
NO COMPANY AND NO PHONE,
TWELVE THE CLOCK DOES CHIME
SO ON EDGE ARE YOU
SITTING ALONE IN THE DARK
WHAT ARE YOU GOING TO DO,
A HORROR MOVIE COMES ON THE TELLY
YOU FEEL THERE'S SOMEONE WITH YOU
YOU HEAR THE SQUEAKY DOOR OPENING
OCH... IT'S ONLY NOSFERATU

BY CATHIE MARTIN

A TIGER. A TIGER

HEY MUMMY WOULD YOU GET ME A TIGER,
THEY'RE BIG CUTE THEY DON'T DRINK CIDER,
THEY'RE YOUR FAVOURITE COLOUR ORANGE AND BLACK,
IF THERE'S NO ROOM IN THE HOUSE I'LL KEEP HIM OUT IN THE BACK,

*A TIGER I THOUGHT THAT'S WHAT YOU SAID,
IT'LL MESS UP THE HOUSE AND MESS UP YOUR BED,
AND WHO'LL LOOK AFTER IT WHEN IT EATS US ALL UP,
I'M TELLING YOU, YOUR BETTER OF WITH A PUP,*

BUT MUMMY THE'RE GIVING THEM AWAY AT THE ZOO,
AND WHEN IT NEEDS THE TOILET IT CAN GO TO THE LOO,
IF ANY ROBBERS BREAK IN IT'LL CHASE THEM AWAY,
SO MUMMY WHAT DO YOU SAY?

*I'LL TELL YOU WHAT I SAY,
YOU CAN ADOPT ONE BUT HERE IT CAN'T STAY,
WHY DON'T I PHONE THE PET SHOP AND ASK THEM FOR A CAT,
COS IT CAN STAY HERE AND YOU CAN FEED IT TIL IT'S FAT,*

BUT MUMMY I DRAW TIGERS ALL THE TIME,
I JUST WISH ONE COULD BE MINE,
IT'LL KEEP YOU COMPANY WHEN I GO TO SCHOOL,
AND MAYBE I COULD EVEN TEACH IT TO PLAY POOL,

*TEACH IT HOW TO PLAY POOL ARE YOU MAD,
NOW YOUR TRYING TO REALLY BE BAD,
NOW GET TO YOUR ROOM AND WATCH TV,
AND COULD YOU PLEASE STOP NAGGING ME,*

SO MUM IS THAT A YES OR A NO,
PLEASE MUM I REALLY NEED TO KNOW,
THE ZOO ARE GIVING THEM AWAY REALLY FAST,
AND I DON'T WANT TO GET THERE LAST,

*OK I GIVE UP, IT'S A YES
YOU BETTER HURRY UP AND GET DRESSED,
AND YOU BETTER START BEHAVING FROM NOW ON,
OR THAT TIGER WILL SOON BE GONE,*

OK, OK I PROMISE TO BEHAVE,
AND I PROMISE TO BATHE,
SO I'M REALLY ALLOWED A TIGER,
OH MUMMY, A TIGER, A TIGER.
(C) SARA THOMSON 1999

COMIC BOOK LIFE

IF LIFE WAS A COMIC BOOK
WHAT SUPERHEROE WOULD YOU BE
IF YOU HAD SUPER POWERS
WHAT WOULD WE SEE?,
WOULD YOU HAVE MYSTIC POWERS
FLOAT AWAY HERE AND THERE
COULD YOU MAKE ULTRASOUND
THAT NO-ONE ELSE COULD HEAR,
WOULD YOU STRETCH A BIT
OR VANISH OUT OF SIGHT
COULD YOU LIFT HEAVY THINGS
COULD YOU GLOW IN THE NIGHT,
WOULD YOU AVENGE WAR
OR WOULD YOU JUDGE AND PERSIST
WOULD YOU BATTLE FOES
OR WOULD YOU RESIST,
YOU'D LIVE A DIFFERENT REALITY
YOU'D GO OUT ON A LIMB
IS THIS CAPRICIOUS
IS THIS JUST A WHIM,
YOU'D BATTLE THRU THIS AND THAT
YOU WOULD BE BOLD AND BRAVE
YOU WOULD SEE ALL THE PEOPLE
THAT YOU WOULD HAVE TO SAVE,
YOU WOULD WEAR A COSTUME
AND WEAR GLOVES TOO
YOU DO BELIEVE IN PEACE
A VERY BIG HEART HAVE YOU,
WOULD YOU BE NUMBER ONE
OR COUNT YOURSELF AS A ZERO
ALL THE HELP THAT YOU'VE GIVEN
YOU CAN COUNT YOURSELF A HERO

BY CATHIE MARTIN

SADNESS

THE PAIN IN YOUR HEART
 YOU DON'T TELL
  WHAT YOU'VE BEEN THROUGH
   YOU HIDE IT WELL

YOU STAY HAPPY
 TO SHOW YOUR STRONG
  BUT DEEP IN YOUR HEART
   YOU KNOW THAT'S WRONG

PEOPLE CAN SEE
 THE SADNESS ON YOUR FACE
  ALTHOUGH YOU CRY
   IT DOESN'T LEAVE A TRACE

YOU FEEL ON YOUR OWN
 AS IF NO-ONE DOTH CARE
  WHY ARE YOU ALONE
   THERE IS NO-ONE THERE

YOU LOOK UP TO THE HEAVENS
 YOUR SANCTUARY IS THERE
  HAPPY THOUGHTS FILL YOUR HEART
   NO MORE SADNESS AND TEAR

BY CATHIE MARTIN

ALONE IN THE PARK

ALONE IN THE PARK
WITH THE LOVE OF MY LIFE
BEING SO CLOSE
TO MY DARLING WIFE

I SIT ON THE SEAT
I SIT HERE ALL DAY
IMAGINING HER CLOSE TO ME
IN HER COMFORTING WAY

I SIT HERE ALL DAY
HOLDING HER HAND
BUT SHE HAS GINE AWAY NOW
TO A BETTER LAND

AS I SIT ALONE
THINKING OF YOU
I REMEMBER THE TIMES
WE USED TO BE TWO

I FEEL SO CLOSE TO HER
AS I SIT HERE ALONE
WHEN IT GETS TIME TO LEAVE
I HEAR A LOW MOAN

WHISPERS IN THE WIND
AS THE WIND PASSES BY
A KISS ON THE CHEEK
A TEAR IN MY EYE

YOU ARE WITH ME ALWAYS
IN MY HEART YOU'LL STAY
I MUST LEAVE NOW
AS YOU'VE GONE AWAY

BY CATHIE MARTIN

WAITING

I LAY HERE AND WAIT FOR HIM I DO
I LAY HERE AND WAIT FOR I KNOW THAT HE'S DUE
I LAY HERE AND WAIT LIKE MY MOTHER BEFORE
I LAY HERE AND WAIT I WAIT FOR HIS SPORE
TO BENIFIT US BOTH HE NEVER LETS US DOWN
HE DOES WHAT HE DOES AND THERES NEVER A FROWN
HONEYS HIS AIM AND WE ALL KNOW HIS GAME
BUT TO ME HES A FRIEND WITHOUT HIM WE'D END

I'M A FLOWER YOU SEE AND HAVE NEED FOR A BEE
SO IF YOU EVER SEE A BEE SAY 'HI MY FRIEND'...'HI FROM ME'

BY CHOW MARTIN

THE HAND

TRIBUTE TO JACK 'KING' KIRBY

THE HAND HAS THE POWER
MORE FOR SOME
TIS' STRONG AND POWERFUL
THE LENDER OF WHICH IT DOES COME,
HOLDING THE BURDEN
THE FUTURE SHALL SEE
THE RESOURCEFULNESS, THE SUCCESS
THE INSPIRATION FROM THEE,
THE WORLD SHALL AWAIT
WHAT THE HAND SHALL GIVE
THE CREATIONS, THE FORTUITY
IN THE MIND SHALL LIVE,
THIS IS THE HAND
FROM WHOEVER IT DOES BELONG
THE PRODUCING, THE CAPABILITY
FROM THE MIGHTY, THE STRONG

BY CATHIE MARTIN

I'M GOING TO DIE AND I'M AFRAID OF THE DARK

AS EACH ONE IS BORN
WE HAVE SO LITTLE TIME TO BLOOM
EVERY MINUTE, HOUR, DAY FADES
SOON THERE IS TO BE GLOOM,
HIDING ALL THE FEELINGS
THAT ONLY I DO KNOW
FEARING THE TIME, THE DARK
WHEN I HAVE TO GO,
WHAT IF I SAID I DIED LAST NIGHT
BUT WAS ALLOWED TO COME BACK TO YOU
I'M SHARING ALL MY LOVE DARLING
PLEASE HELP ME SEE THIS THROUGH,
I WILL COME TO THE END OF LIFES JOURNEY
AND I WON'T STOP DEATH
MEMORIES SHALL LINGER ON BY
I WILL TAKE MY LAST BREATH,
LOVING YOU ALL DEEP IN MY HEART
I'LL TRY AND SAY MY GOODBYE
PLEASE BE HAPPY FROM NOW ON
PLEASE DON'T LIVE LIFE WITH A CRY,
NO LONGER UPON THIS EARTH
I FEAR WHAT IS TO BE
I'M SO SLEEPY MY EYES ARE CLOSING NOW
THE DARKNESS WILL SOON BE UPON ME,
NO-ONE DOTH DIE ALONE
THE HAND OF GOD WILL BE THERE
I SHALL GO WITH A SMILE ON MY LIPS
BUT I SHALL SHED A LONELY TEAR,
MY CLOCK HAS TICKED IT'S LAST TOCK
THE FACE OF DEATH I SEE
GIVE ME DIGNITY AND RECOGNITION
REMEMBER ME

BY CATHIE MARTIN

I LIVED
I LIVED
A WOMAN SHE STANDS AT
THE FOOT OF MY GRAVE,
MY WIFE SHE IS, SHE WAS
ALL THAT I CRAVED
I LOVE HER SO I MISS HER MORE,
I LIE HERE ON MY OWN
SHE'LL JOIN ME I'M SURE,
I LOVED HER FOR YEARS
BEFORE WE MET
WE WERE IN EACH OTHERS WORLD
OUR PATHS WERE SET,
WE WOULD PASS THROUGH TIME
LIVING OUR OWN LIFE,
SHE WOULD DREAM OF A HUSBAND
I WOULD THINK OF A WIFE
WE FINALLY MEET
AND MARRY WE DO,
WE LIVE OUR LIVES TOGETHER
WE SEE THEM ALL THROUGH
THEN ILLNESS HAS TAKEN
ME AWAY FROM MY LIFE,
I SADLY LEAVE MY LOVING WIFE
SO WHILE YOU LIVE BEFORE YOU DECAY
MAKE FRIENDS WITH FAMILY, FRIENDS
AND MAKE IT OKAY.

BY MR CHOW MARTIN

MARY KINGS CLOSE

A historical place
with lots of ghosts
is the Haunting of
Mary Kings Close,
under the buildings
of the royal mile
it's eerie and scary
no one does smile,
near the old Nor Loch
the biogas escaping is very harsh
the spirits go haunting
at the stagnent polluted marsh,
gas may cause hallucinations
but the scare still flows
down in the depths
of Mary Kings Close

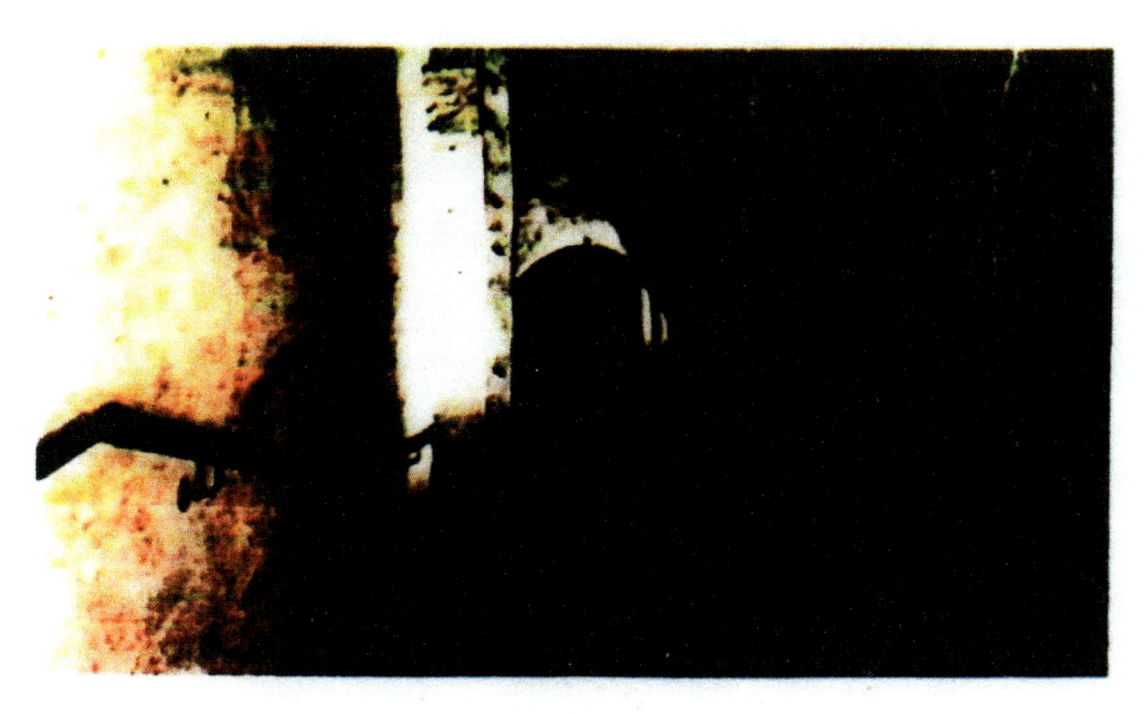

BY CATHIE MARTIN

OOZUM IS SAYING BYE BYE

FUN DAYS AND HAPPY DAYS
EVERY DAY WAS A TREAT
MAKING THE PEOPLE LAUGH
NO MATTER WHO IT WAS WE DID MEET,
SO MUCH JOY TO GIVE
AND SO MUCH JOY TO SHARE
GIVING A BREATH OF UPLIFTMENT
WITH ANYONE WHO WAS THERE,
NOT A SIGN OF NEGATIVITY
THE PURPOSE OF LIFE IS LOVE
HELPING AND GIVING TO OTHERS
A MEANINGFUL LESSON TO BE HEARD OF,
SO TENDER AND LOVING FEELINGS
LOVE FROM THE WARMTH OF THE HEART
THE TIME WILL COME UPON US
WHEN SADLY WE WILL HAVE TO PART,
SADNESS TIMES SO HURTING
THE TEARS WOULD FILL THE EYE
CHERISH EVERY MOMENT
COS.. OOZUM IS SAYING BYE BYE

BY CATHIE MARTIN

TRIBBLES TRIBUTE

SMALL FURRY CREATURES
ALIEN WE BE
GENTLE AND ATTRACTIVE
SO CUTE ARE WE,
NATIVES WE COME FROM
LOTA GEMINORIUM 1V
WE FEED ON PARTICLES OF FOOD
WHICH WE ADORE,
US TRIBBLES ARE BORN PREGNANT
WITH GRAINS OF FOOD WE MULTIPLY
PURRING NOISE WHEN HAPPY
WE MAKE YOU SMILE AND SIGH,

WE DO NOT LIKE KLINGONS
MORTAL ENEMIES ARE THEY
ALL THE HUMAN FOLK
EXUDE LOVE THAT WE SEE,
FEMALE HUMANS
HAVE THE GENTLE TOUCH
SOFT AND LOVING
WE LOVE IT SO MUCH,
YOU'LL CUDDLE UP TO US
SO WE ALL DO CONNECT
OUR COOING SOUND
HAS A TRANQUILIZING EFFECT

BY CATHIE MARTIN

DEATH ROW JETHRO

WHY SHOULD I WORK
AND STRIVE ALL DAY
WHEN A FEW THREATS AND A GUN
WOULD MAKE THEM PAY

YOU STARE DOWN THE BARREL
OF THE GUN IN MY HAND
I'VE GOT TO DO THIS
YOU UNDERSTAND

THE MONEY WAS EASY
THE GETAWAY WAS NOT
COPS ALL AROUND ME
I KNEW I WAS CAUGHT

I SHOULD HAVE RAN FASTER
I SHOULD HAVE BEEN LEAN
BUT I LIKED THE EASY LIFE
YOU KNOW WHAT I MEAN?

MONEY FOR NOTHING
BUT NOW I MUST PAY
THE JUDGE AND THE JURY
HAVE HAD THE LAST SAY

WITH GUN IN MY HAND
I WAS ON A HIGH
I WAIT ON DEATH ROW NOW
I'M GOING TO DIE

THE CHAIR IS THERE
IT'S WAITING FOR ME
NO MORE WILL I LIVE
NO MORE WILL I BE

BY CATHIE MARTIN

BABY WENT ROCK-A-BYE

HUSH MY LITTLE DARLING
SLEEPY TIME FOR YOU
PLAYTIME IS ALL OVER
COSY BED YOU GOT TO GO TO,
ALL THE DAY LONG
YOU HAD SUCH FUN
YOU WOULD CRAWL AROUND THE FLOOR
YOU ALSO WALKED AND TRIED TO RUN,
TIMELESS TIMES SO ENCHANTING
WITH ALL THE LOVE OF THE DAY
ALWAYS FOREVER A MEMORY
WITH US ALL IT WILL STAY,
ROCK-A-BYE MY SWEET BABY
IT'S NOW TIME TO DREAM
BEDDY BAWS WITH TEDDY
CUDDLE UP SO WARM AND SERENE
ROCK-A-BYE MY BABY
ROCK AWAY ALL THE BLUES
CLOSE YOUR EYES MY DARLING
TIME FOR YOU TO SNOOZE

BY CATHIE MARTIN

HERO

A POLICE DOG
I AM I BE
IF THERE IS TROUBLE
I DO GET SET FREE,
I DO AS I'M TOLD
POLICING WHEN IT DOES MATTER
I HAVE A STRONG BITE
YOUR BONES I WILL SHATTER,
DON'T BE BAD OR CRUEL
I'LL GET SET ON YOU
THEN YOU'LL BE SORRY
YOU DO WHAT YOU DO,
POLICING IS MY LIFE
I AM SO PROUD TO BE A NAME
THIS JOB IS NOT FOR FUN
IT IS NOT JUST A GAME,
FIGHTING CRIMES I DO
SAVING WHEN IN NEED
I AM OF FLESH, BLOOD AND BONE
LIKE YOU I DO BLEED,
I CAN SNIFF OUT BAD THINGS
TOO MANY TO NAME
DOING MY IMPORTANT JOB
THAT IS MY AIM,
I AM BUTCH THE POLICE DOG
I GET MY JOB DONE
HAPPY..YES I AM
SORROWS I HAVE NONE

BY CATHIE MARTIN

EDINBURGH DUNGEON

IN EDINBURGH CASTLE
IN THE DUNGEONS BELOW
THERE ARE PRISONS THERE
THAT NOT MANY PEOPLE KNOW,
VOICES OF THE CAPTURED
SHADOWS OF THE PAST
GHOSTS OF THE UNFORTUNATE
THE HAUNTING TIMES LAST,
THE IRON GATE OF THE CASTLE
SHUTS THE HEAVENS OUT
YOU CAN'T HEAR PRISONERS SCREAM
YOU CAN'T HEAR THEM SHOUT,
SHUT AWAY IN THE DARK
NO ONE DOTH KNOW
BURIED DEEP AND DANK
SO THEIR BODIES DON'T SHOW,
VISITORS DO GO THERE
IN ALL KIND OF WEATHER
THE SPIRITS CAN'T ESCAPE
THEY GATHER TOGETHER,
THE PHANTOM BAGPIPER BOY
THE PRISONERS OF WAR
THE HEADLESS DRUMMER
THERE ARE ALSO MORE
WITCHES HAVE BEEN BROUGHT HERE
TORTURED AND KILLED
GHOSTLY WORKMEN ARE SEEN
MAKING EVERYONE CHILLED
THE GHOST OF A DOG
WANDERS THE DOG CEMETERY
APPARITIONS AND ORBS
EDINBURGH DUNGEONS ARE LEGENDARY

BY CATHIE MARTIN

PUSSYCAT

'CAN I HAVE A PUSSYCAT
SO SOMETHING WITH ME WILL PLAY
THAT WOULD MAKE ME HAPPY
THAT WOULD MAKE MY DAY'.
'THAT'S A GOOD IDEA
YES WE'LL BUY A CAT
YOU CAN PLAY GAMES
MAYBE TEACH IT THIS AND THAT'
'YEAH! I WILL CALL IT PET
THAT'S A NICE NAME
IT'LL MAKE ME HAPPY
WHEN WE TAKE IT HAME'
'YOU'LL NEED TO LOOK AFTER IT
TALK TO IT ALL THE TIME
CLEAN UP ALL IT'S BUISNESS
SAY GOODNIGHT AT BEDTIME'
'I REALLY LIKE THAT ONE
PLEASE BUY IT FOR ME
I PROMISE TO BE GOOD
I'LL BEHAVE, YOU'LL SEE'
'DON'T BE SILLY DARLING
THAT'S NOT A PUSSYCAT
IT'LL BE A STRONG TIGER
WE CAN'TY BUY YOU THAT
IT WILL GROW AND GROW
IT NEEDS A SPACIOUS HABITAT
FORGET THIS BABY TIGER
WEE'LL BUY A STRIPED PUSSYCAT
MORE CUDDLY FOR YOU
IT WILL LOOK THE SAME
YOU CAN STILL KEEP THE LOVELY 'PET' NAME'
OH THANK YOU DARLING DADDY
I APPRECIATE THAT
IT WON'T BE A BABY TIGER
BUT IT WILL BE MY PUSSYCAT'

BY CATHIE MARTIN

VISITOR

THE FOUR WALLS ARE MY PRISON
I FEEL NOTHING BUT GLOOM
IS THIS TO BE MY SANCTUARY
OR IS THIS MY DOOM
I HEAR LOTS OF NOISES
BUT FACES I DON'T SEE
THERE IS NO-ONE AROUND
THERE'S JUST MY SHADOW AND ME
I HEAR MY HEART BEATING
AM I ALIVE OR DEAD
CAN I ESCAPE OUTSIDE
NO WAY...I'D BE AFRAID
I PRAY TO THE HEAVEN ABOVE
WHEN I'M DOWN FEELING LOW
SAME TIME EVERY DAY
THERE'S A NOISE AT MY WINDOW
I MAKE OUT A SHADOW
BUT MY EYES ARE ALL BLURRED
MY ONE AND ONLY VISITOR
IS A TINY LITTLE BIRD

BY CATHIE MARTIN

THE SCARE WITHIN

THE HANDS OF THE WANTING
THE CRIES OF THE NEED BE
THE BODIES OF THE ILL
IN THE WORLD FOR US ALL TO SEE,

BELIEF IS A SHADOW OF DOUBT
HOPE AND FAITH ARE BLIND
A GIVING A MUST FOR TO DO
THE HELPING AND WHY ARE IN MIND,

A VAST OPEN SPACE TO SHARE
WITH LIVING BETWIXT AND BETWEEN
THE HONOUR OF HAVING A LIFE
THE BEST WONDERMENT I'VE EVER SEEN,

THE FEAR IN ME TO WHAT WILL
THE SCARE OF IT IS GOING TO BE
THE FRIGHT OF WHEN AND WHY
THE HORROR THAT WILL OVERCOME ME

BY CATHIE MARTIN

SANTA

ART BY MR CHOW MARTIN

SANTA WISHES YOU ALL
 A MERRY YEAR
  THROWING YOU A SNOWBALL
   WITH A HAPPY CHEER
    WHERE IS SANTAS HELPERS
     ON THIS COLD NIGHT
      SANTA IS READY
       FOR A SNOWBALL FIGHT
        SANTA WILL VISIT
         COMING FROM THE NORTH
          SPREADING FUN AND LAUGHTER
           FROM THIS DAY FORTH

BY CHOW MARTIN

AS THE FLOODING HELL CAME..

When the water came in
Lost is the world as I once knew it.
The moon stands still and the destruction rages -
The mother screamed, then I didn't see or hear her anymore -
The cattle, it cries, the dog drowns and I -
I saved my life when the world sank all around -
The water rolls and flows, takes everything along,
it breaks my life,, what I love
Lost and good and I lost myself
Words fall, they don't comfort, actions follow, they don't help
In my pain I am alone, faint and still -
The eyes, they are tearless -
I'm not crying anymore.
And the world? Soon she won't care, the misfortune becomes commonpl
©Frauke Danker 19.07..2021
Paint: ©Frauke Danker

BY FRAUKE DANKER

BABY BABY BUT WHAT'S INSIDE

MY GENES DO SLUMBER
BUT TOMORROW I KILL
THE CURE IS NOT THERE
I WILL DO AS I WILL

CUTE AS A BABY
A BABY I BE
I'M ALL YOU EVER WANTED
YOU SEE EVERYTHING IN ME

I GARGLE AS CUTE AS CUTE AS CAN BE
I SMILE I LAUGH ATTENTION I SEEK
I'M A KILLER YOU SEE BUT NOT QUITE RIPE YET
WHEN I REACH MATURITY THE OUTLOOK IS BLEAK

THE SIGNS ARE NOT THERE
WHERE COULD THEY BE
THE KILLER IS HIDING
PLAYING ON YOUR KNEE

       BY MR CHOW MARTIN

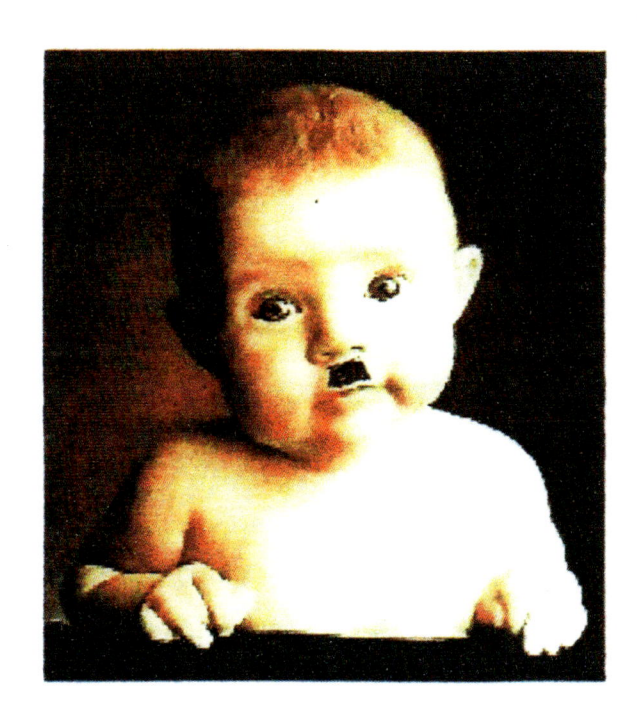

BY CHOW MARTIN

ALL IS ONE

WHO ARE YOU
MY DEAR
TWILIGHTS....?
I DON'T KNOW
THE FIRST, THE LAST
AND EVER SO.....
WHERE ARE WE?
HERE
WHY ASK....?
ALTHOUGH YOU OUGHT TO GO
THOUGH NOT BACK TO THE DREAMING
YOUR A DIFFERENT KIND OF LANGUAGE
SO WITH CLEAR VOICE YOUR HEART AND SPEAK
IN SILENT SIGHS
THINK ONE IS ALL
AS THE RIVER REFLEX THE MOON
AND THE MOON REFLEX THE SUN
ALL IS ONE
LOVE THAT WHITE LIGHT IT NEVER FADES
YET FEW MORTAL HEARTS WILL EVER KNOW

BY COLIN HOPKINS

THE ACRASIAL SPIRIT

FULL OF AMARULENCE AND WOE
THE VENGEFULNESS DOES ARISE
THIS SPIRIT OF SOMETHING
ACTS OUT AND DOING BEFORE YOUR EYES,
THE HAPPENINGS ARE SO WRONGFUL
MAKING YOU SO TRISTIFICAL
WHELMING UP WITH UNSURITY
THE EYES WATER, THE TEARS DO TRICKLE,
THE UNTEMPERING OF THE PRESENCE
YOU DARE NOT QUAIL
REACHES YOU TO THE LIMITS
THIS YOU CANNOT UNVEIL,
THE TEPMPERENCE OF THE ERRATIC BEING
SHALL HAUNT ON FOREVER AND A DAY
IN YOUR SOUL YOUR MIND
THE VISITANT WITH YOU SHALL STAY

BY CATHIE MARTIN

EXPLOSIVE EXPRESSION OF LOVE

ART BY ROMEO TANGHAL Sr

I'LL AWAKEN YOUR FEELINGS
OF DEEP LOVE INSIDE
THE DESIRES, THE PASSION
OUR HANDS TOGETHER WILL SLIDE,
HOLDING EACH OTHER CLOSE
WE LOVE EACH OTHER SO
OUR HEARTFELT LOVE
WE CAN ALWAYS SHOW,
OVERWHELMED WITH DELIGHT
WITH THE CARESSNESS, THE TOUCH
STROKES OF AFFECTION
THE HEAT IS SO MUCH,
LOST IN THE MOMENT TOGETHER
THE FUN OF IT ALL
THE GAMES PLAYED TOGETHER
WE DO HAVE A BALL,
ALWAYS TOGETHER
LOVING ME, LOVING YOU
OUR HEARTS ARE ENTWINED
THE SWEETNESS HAS GREW AND GREW

POEM BY CATHIE MARTIN

YESTERDAY I TAUGHT THE BIRDS TO SING...

YESTERDAY I TAUGHT THE BIRDS TO SING
YESTERDAY WHEN HAPPINESS WAS MY THING

ALL PLEASURE HAS LEFT ME, SO SICK AND UNWELL
EVERY DAY OF MY LIFE NOW IS A STRUGGLE
THROUGH HELL

I NOW WANT TO DIE I KNOW THAT I DO
I WISH I KNEW WHERE ALL THE GOOD TIMES WENT TO

THE BIRDS NOW ARE SILENT, IT'S MY HEARING
YOU KNOW
THE DAY WILL COME SOON LIFE I WILL LET GO

I BARE YOU NO MALICE I BARE YOU NO WOE
IT'S SIMPLY MY TIME, MY TIME TO GO..

BY CHOW MARTIN

LOVE OF YOUR FEATHERED FREINDS

ART BY COOPER DRACONIAN

YOUR
LITTLE FEATHERED
FRIEND TOUCHES YOUR H
EART WITH THEIR LOVE AND TH
EIR COMMITMENT TO STAY BY
YOU AND NEVER PART, ALWAY
S BE WITH YOU EVERY NIGHT AN
D DAY WHISTLE, CHIRP AND SINGING
IN A MOST HAPPY WAY, HOPE AND TRUS
T ALWAYS BELIEVING IN YOU TRUSTING E
VERYTHING FOR THEM THAT YOU DO, THE
Y APPRECIATE THE TIME AND THE TALKING T
O THEM THE SWEETNESS, THE UNKNOWN, TH
E JOY THAT IS SHARED THIS COMPANIONSHIP
JUST CAN'T BE COMPAIRED, THE DELIGHT THE
INSPIRATION THE ESTEEMED BEAUTY THE FREE
DOM OF THE HEART LIVING DAY BY DAY TELLIN
G YOU THANKS IN THEIR OWN WAY, HAPPY T
O BE ALIVE IT'S A DELIGHT TO BE OUR EMO
TIONS INSIDE NO-ONE CAN SEE WE C
RY,WE DO HURT WE ALL LOVE TO
BE FREE, WE LOVE ATTENTION
WE LOVE TO BE HEARD
WE WILL MAKE A
NOISE TO GET
YOU OUT YO
UR BED LO
VE THAT
IS SHAE
ED BY Y
OU AN
D BY
ME A
LOV
ING
TH
IN
G T
O S
EE

POEM BY CATHIE MARTIN

AT LAST

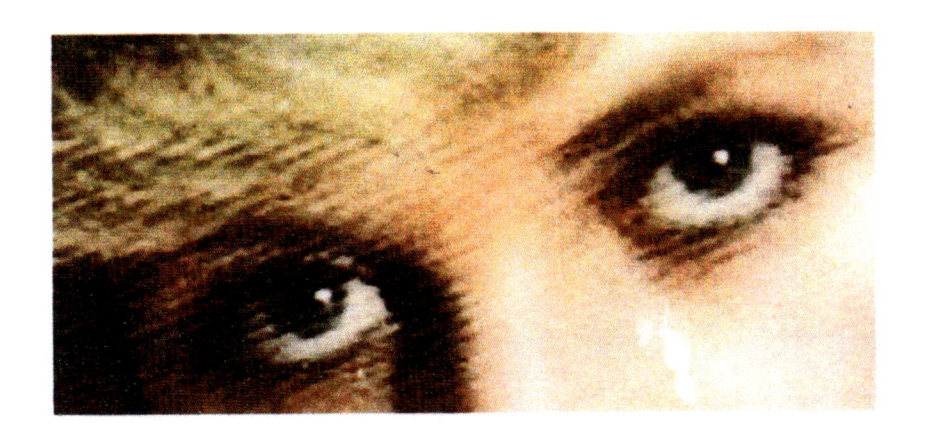

AS
MY T
EARS FA
LL ALL MY
EMOTIONS DO
WEARY, I CRY
WITHIN MYSELF TH
AT NO-ONE CAN HEAR,
NO LOVE SHALL BE AMISS
IF I HAVE NO-ONE TO TELL N
O-ONE TO DEPEND UPON AND
NO-ONE TO HOLD, I THOUGHT
THERE WAS A TOMORROW, A F
UTURE OF HEAVENLY DREAMS, BU
T MY LIFE CAME TO AN END THAT N
O-ONE DOES BELIEVE, I AM AT COMFO
RT NOW WITH THE ONE WHO DOES TRU
ST AND HOLDS MY HEART, MY HAPPIN
ESS AT LAST WITH SMILES I CAN SHARE
NO MORE SORROW, LOVE FOREVER M
ORE SHALL BE MINE, AT PEACE, NO
MORE PAIN OR HATE TO BE
I AM AT PEACE AT LAST

BY UNKNOWN

A FORTUNE OF GOLD

A PROMISE BINDS
ALL OUR HEARTS TOGETHER
ON THE PATH WE DO STAY
FORGET OR REGRET...NEVER,
THE TRUTH OF LOVE
IS A FORTUNE OF GOLD
THE FEELINGS OF CONTEMPT
THE HEART DOES SO HOLD,
THE DESTINY OF LIFE
HOW SWEET THE KISS
A LOVE THAT'S RARE
IN IT'S ETERNAL BLISS,
NEVER TO SAY ADIEU
SMILE AND SAY HELLO
THE UNDERSTANDING OF TOMORROW
IS NEVER TO LET GO,
WE WILL STAY TOGETHER
WILL IT BE SO WRONG
ALWAYS AND FOREVER
WE WILL GROW SO STRONG,
THE PERFECTION OF LIFE
IS LIVING WITH YOU
THE WRONG TO THE RIGHT
WE WILL SEE IT THROUGH,
THE FORTUNE OF GOLD
NEVER TO BE SEEN
THE INTENSIONS ARE TRUE
BELIEVE IN THE DREAM

BY CATHIE MARTIN

THE BEES IN THE KNOW

THE LITTLE BEE
LIVES FOR TOMORROW
IT IS HAPPY
NO TIME FOR SORROW
IT WHISPERS TO ME
WHERE IT GOES
IT TELLS ME
WHAT IT SEES AND DOES
IT TELLS OF THE CHILDREN
THAT PLAY GAMES
CATCHING THE BEES
AND GIVING THEM NAMES
WE LAND ON A FLOWER
AND LEAVE A SCENT BEHIND
THIS TELLS THE OTHER BEES
NO NECTAR WILL THEY FIND
WE ARE YOUR LITTLE FRIEND
WE DON'T MEAN ANY HARM
NO MALICE WE INTEND
WHEN SEEING US KEEP CALM
WE EAT THE NECTAR
THE FLOWERS DO GIVE
WE HELP POLLINATE THE LAND
SO THINGS MAY LIVE
BUZZ BUZZING ABOUT
IN THE WARM SUN RAYS
NOT HAVING A LONG LIFE SPAN
WE HAVE TO ENJOY OUR DAYS
FUZZY LITTLE CREATURE
YELLOW AND BLACK
WE WILL GATHER TOGETHER
DON'T BE TAKEN ABACK

BY CATHIE MARTIN

FROZEN TEARS

THE HEART IS SO HURT
THE TEARS ARE ALL FROZEN
WRESTLING WITH THE MIND
YOUR FEELINGS ARE TAUT, YOU CANNOT LOOSEN,
ALONE IN THE NIGHT
ALONE IN THE DAY
SEARCHING FOR SOMEONE
TO SHOW YOU THE WAY,
A PITY, A SHAME
YOU CRY INSIDE, YOU FEEL BROKE
SADNESS HAS OVERCOME
YOUR LIVING, YOUR LIFE, JUST A JOKE,
TRYING TO MOVE ON
BUT BLINDED BY THE PAIN
YOUR EMOTIONS ARE SUPPRESSED
WHAT IS THERE FOR YOU TO GAIN,
THE HURT ONCE AGAIN
A THOUSAND TIMES WITH A BROKEN HEART
THE TEARS ARE ALL FROZEN
WHEN WILL THEY FALL, WHEN WILL THEY START,
TO SEEK YET TO FIND
LIVING THROUGH THE YEARS
YOU CAN'T CRY, YOU CAN'T SHOW
THE SEASONS OF TEARS

BY CATHIE MARTIN

POOCH

ART BY PAUL ELDRIDGE

WITH CHARMS TO CHEER YOUR HEART
A FRIEND FOR LIFE I WILL BE
TO CONVEY THE LOVE BACK TO YOU
THAT YOU GIVE TO ME,
I'LL BE BY YOU DAY AND NIGHT
I'LL WATCH AND PLAY GAMES TOO
I KNOW WHAT IS A RIGHT THING
I ALSO KNOW WHAT IS TABOO,
CARE FOR ME MY FRIEND
A LOVING DOG SURELY SURE I'LL BE
I'M WELL BEHAVED I PROMISE
YOU LOVE ME? YOUR GONNA KEEP ME? WHOOPIE!!

POEM BY CATHIE MARTIN

HAPPY MERRY TIME

THE MAGIC OF FUN
   IS A WONDEROUS THING
      BEING JOYFUL WITH SMILES
         AN UPLIFTING FEELING YOU WANT TO SING,

HAPPINESS CAN BE INFECTIOUS
   SHARE ALL YOUR CHEER
      PASS IT AROUND WITH A GRIN OR SMILE
      KEEP IT GOING EVERY YEAR,

GOD BLESS EACH YEAR
   UPON US THEY DO COME
      BE HAPPY WITH YOUR NEIGHBOUR
         TREAT THEM AS YOUR CHUM,

A SENSE OF HARMONIES
   WITH LAUGHTER, RAIN, SNOW AND SNOWBALL
      EVERY BREATH IS OF GLEE
         GOOD WILL TO ALL

BY AVRIL GRAY

INSIDE MY HEAD

THE DEPTH OF THE BEGINING
IF WE COULD ONLY SEE
THE BOUNDARY OF THOUGHTS
WHAT WILL OCCUR, WHAT WILL BE,
THE PREFRONTAL CORTEX INSIDE MY HEAD IS A POET
BOUNCING WORDS BACK AND FORTH
CONTINUOUS IT IS ALL OF THE TIME
AND THERE WILL BE A NEW BIRTH,
THE DEVELOPEMENT OF SURPRISE
WILL BE A GREAT OUTCOME
THINKING AND PRODUCING
WHERE DO THE WORDS COME FROM,
TO NUTURE AND TO TEND
BRINGING TO LIFE WHAT IS DORMANT
THE ENJOYMENT OF SUGGESTIONS AND METAPHORS
TO BRING US ALL INTO THE MOMENT,

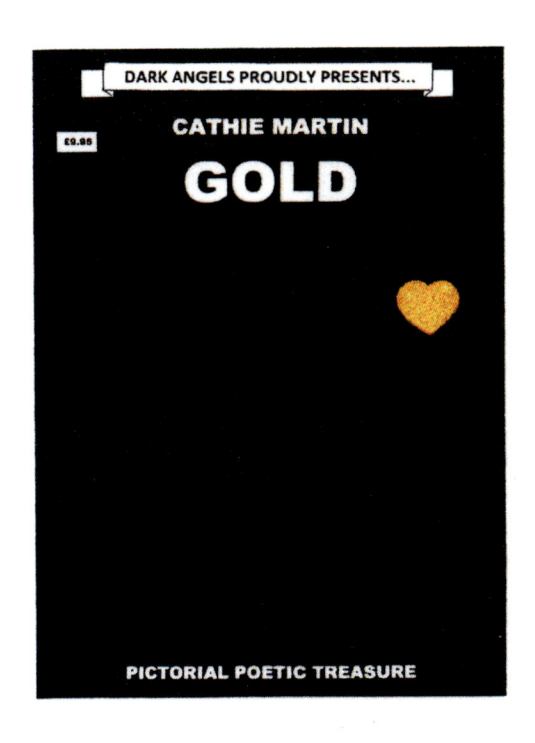

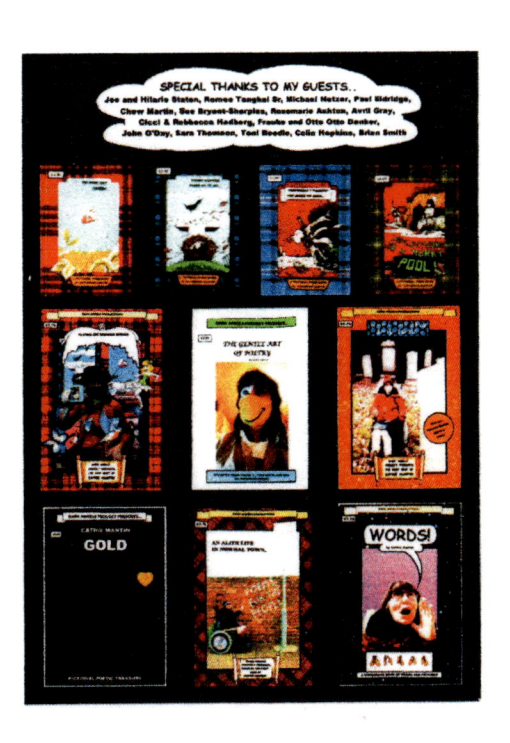

POEM BY CATHIE MARTIN, ART BY MR CHOW MARTIN

TALK TO ME DAWGGIE!!

IF YOU DON'T TELL ME WHAT YOU THINK
HOW AM I TO KNOW
TALK TO ME DAWGGIE
COS I LOVE YOU SO

I'LL LISTEN DEEPLY
SHARE YOUR THOUGHTS WITH ME
TALK TO ME DAWGGIE
IT IS SO VERY EASY

MAYBE YOUR SHY
AND YOU DON'T WANT TO SAY
BUT TALK TO ME DAWGGIE
I WON'T GO AWAY

I SEE IN YOUR EYES
YOU HAVE THINGS ON YOUR MIND
TALK TO ME DAWGGIE
IN ME YOU CAN CONFIDE

POEM BY CATHIE MARTIN INSPIRED BY CHOW MARTIN

GO TELL YOUR MOTHER ALL ABOUT IT

IF THINGS HAPPEN TO YOU
YOU WOULD LIKE SOMEONE TO KNOW
TO SHARE ALL YOUR WORRIES
ALL THE HURT THAT MIGHT SHOW

DON'T HIDE YOUR EMOTIONS
DON'T PLAY ABOUT WITH WORDS
SAY WHAT'S ON YOUR MIND
NO MATTER HOW ABSURB

GO TELL YOUR MOTHER
SHE WILL UNDERSTAND
IF YOU NEED HELP IN ANYWAY
SHE WILL GIVE YOU A GUIDING HAND

DON'T KEEP THINGS LOCKED AWAY AND HIDDEN
DON'T KEEP THINGS PRIVATE
DON'T LEAVE IT TILL IT'S TOO LATE
GO TELL YOUR MOTHER ALL ABOUT IT

BY CATHIE MARTIN INSPIRED BY CHOW MARTIN

GREYFRIARS BOBBY

THE MOST SELFLESS WEE DOG
WITH A VERY WARM HEART
STAYED BY HIS MASTERS SIDE
AND WOULD NEVER PART
AN EDINBURGH BOBBY
HIS NAME WAS JOHN GRAY
WAS BURIED IN GREYFRIARS KIRK
THE WEE DAWGGIE WOULD LAY
NOT LEAVING HIS MASTER
THIS WEE SKYE TERRIER DOG
IN ALL KINDS OF WEATHER
THE SUN, RAIN, SNOW, FOG
FOR 14 LONG YEARS
THE DAWGGIE STOOD GUARD
HE WAITED FOR HIS MASTER
THROUGH THE YEARS SO HARD
THESE FAITHFUL COMPANIONS
THE LOVE WAS SO DEEP
WHEN OLD JOCK DIED
THE WEE TERRIER DID WEEP
BUT BEING SO LOYAL
SO LOVINGINGLY BRAVE
THE WEE BLACK DOG
DIED ON HIS MASTERS GRAVE

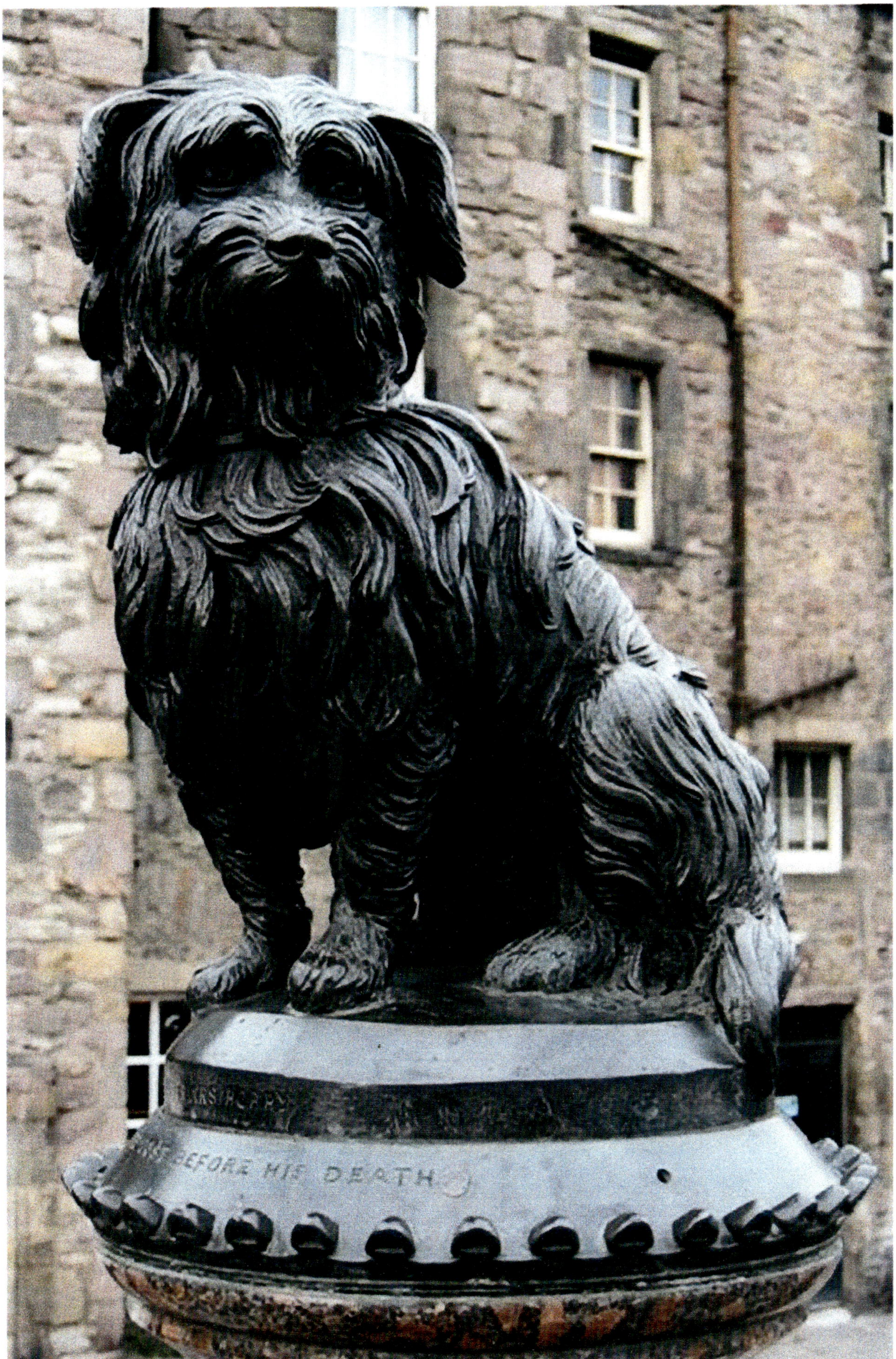
BEFORE HIS DEATH

WAITING FOR THE END

I AM WAITING ALONE
AS THE WORLD PASSES ME BY
NO POINT IN LIVING
NO REASON TO CRY,
NO-ONE KNOWS WHEN THE END IS NIGH
TO MUCH FOR US TO COPE
EMPTINESS, DARKNESS, ALONENESS
MOTIONLESS WITH NO HOPE,
THE APOCOLYPSE OF THE WORLD
NO MORE FOR ANYONE TO SEE
THE SUFFERING, THE DIEING
WHAT WILL BE WILL BE,

ART BY MR CHOW MARTIN

DESTRUCTIONS WE MADE
THERE'S A PRICE WE MUST PAY
JOURNEY TO THE END
NO MORE NIGHT OR DAY,
OUR PLANET IS DIEING
THAT I CAN SEE
THE WORLD AROUND ME
HAS BEEN RUINED BY YOU AND ME,
MOTHER NATURES HAD ENOUGH
IT IS FIGHTING BACK AS WE CAN SEE
OUR PLIGHT IS HOPELESS, THE CAUSE IS LOST
THERE WILL BE NO MORE HAPPINESS, THERE WILL BE NO MORE GLEE

BY CATHIE AND CHOW MARTIN

MY TIGER LOVE

I'M A TIGER OF LOVE
A BEAST OF BEAUTY
MY HEART IS FEIRCE BUT KIND
THAT IS MY DUTY,
I AM A CUDDLY CREATURE
COLOURS SPECTACULAR TOO
I NEED MY FREEDOM AS WELL
I DON'T BELONG IN A ZOO,

ART BY COOPER DRACONIA

I COULD BE STALKING
SNEEKING UP ON YOU
BUT I AM WARM AND CUDDLY
I JUST WANT TO PLAY LIKE YOU DO,
MAYBE A CUDDLY TOY
WITH EYES SHINY AND BRIGHT
TAKE ME HOME WITH YOU
CUDDLE UP TO ME AT NIGHT

POEM BY CATHIE MARTIN

OUR TIME TOGETHER

HOLD ME TIGHT, ALL THOUGH THE NIGHT
LET ME FEEL THE WARMTH OF YOUR HEART
CUDDLES FROM YOU, FROM ME TO YOU TOO
WITH THE LOVE THAT NO-ONE CAN PART

NOTHING CAN COMPARE
THERE'S NOTHING AS SWEET AS YOU
MY DREAM, MY ROCK, MY LIFE
MY LOVE MY DARLING SO TRUE,

TIME TOGETHER IS PRECIOUS
ALL THE TIME WE WILL ALWAYS BE
HOLDING THE HEART OF THE OTHER
DEEP DOWN WITHIN FOR THE WORLD TO SEE

EXPCTATIONS THAT WE WOULD BELONG
DEEP LOVE, TRUE LOVE WAS THERE
WE SEARCHED , WE FOUND, WE GOT EACH OTHER
OUR LIFE WE WILL ALWAYS SHARE

BY CATHIE MARTIN

A LITTLE RAY OF SUNSHINE

A LITTLE RAY OF SUNSHINE
IS JUST WHAT YOU ARE
YOUR LOVING SMILE WILL HELP
YOU GO FAR,

YOUR MOTHER I AM
I'LL ALWAYS BE
THERE FOR YOU ALWAYS
YOU MEAN SO MUCH TO ME,

AS CHILDHOOD LEAVES YOU AND
YOU ENTER THE WORLD
REMEMBER YOUR SMILE
AND MAKE ME SO PROUD

BY CATHIE MARTIN

HOKAY BOYS!!

EVERYBODY WANTS TO BE SOMEBODY
YOU WANT TO BE AS BIG AS ME
I'M THE BOSS AROUND HERE
I'M THE BOSS ..SEE!!,
YOUR GONNA TAKE ORDERS
YOUR GONNA LISTEN TO ME
I WANT QUIETNESS AROUND HERE
QUIETNESS I SAID ... SEE,
I'M THE KING OF THE WORLD
NOBODY LAUGHS AT ME
HOKAY BOYS WHADDYA WANT
SOMETHING FOR BEING GOOD FROM ME,
TIME TO SAY MY PRAYERS MUGS
IT'S BED TIME FOR ME
I'M STILL THE BOSS RIGHT
THE BOSS..THAT'S ME.. SEE

BY CATHIE MARTIN

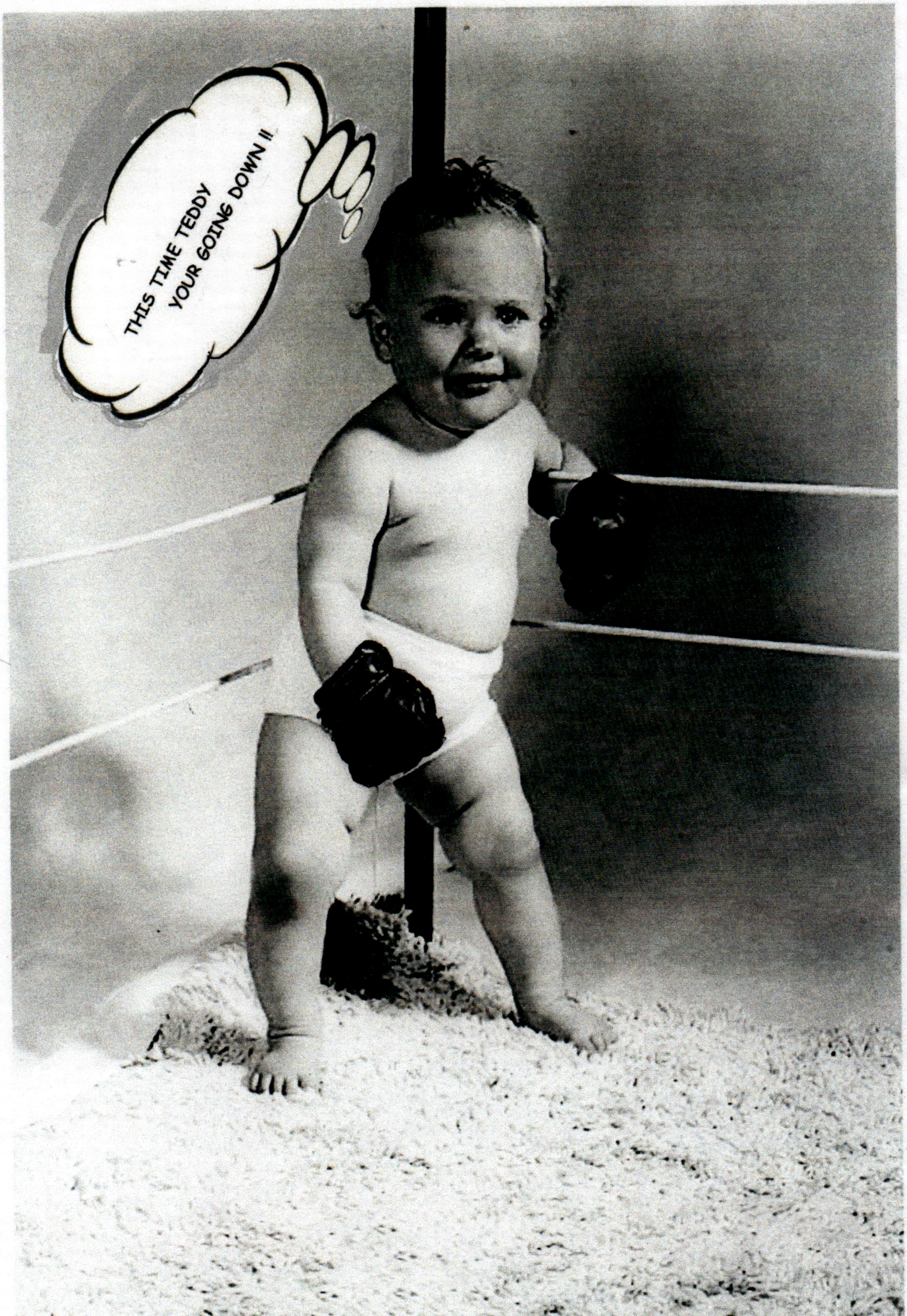
THIS TIME TEDDY
YOUR GOING DOWN !!

EVERYTHING MUST END

ALL THINGS COME TO AN END
THEY CAN'T GO ON FOREVER
THE TIME, THE PLACE THE WANTING
MAY NOT BE YOURS, NEVER,

WHO MISSES THE PRECIOUS MOMENTS
OF LIFE PRESENT NOW AND PAST
A NIGHTMARE, A BEAUTY, A MYSTERY
THE TIME HAS GONE SO FAST,

The End

FROM EACH PAGE IN LIFE
DELIGHTS AND WISDOM SO
CHANGES AND HAPPENINGS AS YOU GO ALONG
THE THINGS THAT HAVE TO GO,

AT THE END OF LIFES JOURNEY
THE JOY, THE LOVE SO TRUE
YOU'LL HAVE THE PERFECT ENDING
THE BEST OF THINGS FOR YOU

BY CATHIE MARTIN